THE SON OF ZEBEDEE

THE
SON OF ZEBEDEE

AND THE FOURTH GOSPEL

BY

THE REV. H. P. V. NUNN, M.A.

WITH A PREFACE BY

THE MOST REV. W. TEMPLE, D.D.

ARCHBISHOP OF YORK

LONDON
SOCIETY FOR PROMOTING
CHRISTIAN KNOWLEDGE
LONDON: NORTHUMBERLAND AVENUE, W.C.2

First Published, 1927
New Edition, 1932

PATRIS

QUI IPSE INTEGROS FONTES SEMPER HAURIENS

OMISSIS HUMANÆ FALSI NOMINIS SCIENTIÆ TURBIDIS RIVULIS

ALIOS EXEMPLO DOCTRINA SCRIPTIS

IDEM FACERE DOCEBAT

MEMORIÆ DEDICATUM

PREFACE

BY THE ARCHBISHOP OF YORK

I REGARD it a great honour that Mr. Nunn should have asked me to write a preface to this short but impressive study of a most important subject. Mr. Nunn is a scholar well qualified to help us in clearing our minds about a matter on which I find myself convinced that prejudice has obscured the judgment of even great authorities. The constant controversy about the origin of the Fourth Gospel illustrates the difficulty of reaching a conclusion when the arguments upon the two sides do not meet and set up a resultant direction for the mind to follow, but, on the contrary, fail to meet each other at all, and sway to and fro ineffectively. The first necessity is to get back to the facts that have any bearing on the question. This, Mr. Nunn, with his great lucidity and wide knowledge, helps us to do, and thereby places all who are interested in this important question under a great obligation.

Mr. Nunn has added a criticism of the section in Canon Streeter's book, *The Four Gospels*, which deals with the Fourth Gospel. I have the greatest admiration for Canon Streeter's work, but had myself felt that this section was below the level of the rest. Readers of that book who follow Mr. Nunn's critique will be supplied with the materials for a judgment.

W. EBOR.

PREFACE TO SECOND EDITION

A SECOND edition of this book having been called for, the author has added to the two essays in the first edition a short chapter on recent criticism of the Gospel.

Those who wish for further information on the matters discussed in this book will find it in Dr. Nolloth's *The Fourth Evangelist*, and in M. Lepin's *L'origine du Quatrième Evangile* and his *La valeur historique du Quatrième Evangile*, both published by Letouzey et Ané of Paris. The general question of the bearing of modern criticism on all the Gospels is well treated in M. Lepin's later book, *Le Christ Jésus*, published by Bloud et Gay of Paris, and at much greater length in Father de Grandmaison's *Jésus Christ*, an English translation of which is being published by Sheed and Ward. The late Bishop Gore's little book on Jesus Christ also briefly deals with this problem.

H. P. V. NUNN.

"The truth is that the criticism of the Fourth Gospel on the liberal side has become largely conventional; one writer after another repeats certain stereotyped formulæ without testing them. It is high time that they were really tested and confronted with the facts."—PROFESSOR SANDAY, *Criticism of the Fourth Gospel.*

WAS JOHN THE SON OF ZEBEDEE A MARTYR?

UNTIL recently the residence of John, the son of Zebedee, in Asia and his death there were assumed to be among the best attested facts in ancient Church history.

During the last few years, however, some evidence has been brought forward by certain German critics, such as Schwartz and Wellhausen, which is alleged to prove that he never was in Asia; but that he was put to death by the Jews in Palestine, probably at an early date.

This evidence is accepted as conclusive by certain British scholars such as Dr. Moffatt in his *Introduction to the Literature of the New Testament*, Dr. Charles in his *Commentary on the Revelation*, and Dr. Burney in his *Aramaic Origin of the Fourth Gospel*. In fact, it is fast becoming "one of the assured results of criticism."

The question raised by this theory is not an unimportant one, because, if the Apostle John never was in Asia, it not only becomes almost impossible to regard him as the actual author of the Fourth Gospel, but it also follows that his teaching and recollections can no longer be regarded as its source and inspiration. The Gospel is deprived not only of an apostolic author, but also of the authority and prestige that it might derive from being the product of a church and a school of thought over which an Apostle once presided.

To those to whom it is almost an *articulus stantis aut cadentis ecclesiæ* that the Fourth Gospel could not possibly have been written by an immediate follower of Christ, this theory is naturally most welcome.

It settles the question. " Dead men tell no tales," and Apostles who died hundreds of miles from the place where the Gospel is generally acknowledged to have been written, and long before any one supposes that it was written, cannot have had any part in it.

It commends itself also to those critics who, while not prepared to grant that the portrait of Jesus in the Fourth Gospel is nothing more than an embodied projection of the spiritual experience of the Church of the early second century, find it difficult to believe that the Gospel can have been written by a man of the antecedents and training of the son of Zebedee.

In his *Commentary on the Revelation* Dr. Charles has set out briefly, and apparently very cogently, the evidence for the alleged early and violent death of the Apostle. We recommend those who wish to see how the question is treated by a modern writer to refer to pp. xlv.-l. of that work.

The evidence which has hitherto been held sufficient to prove the residence of the Apostle John in Asia is as follows :

Irenæus, Bishop of Lyons, who was born in Asia about A.D. 140 and lived at least until the end of the century, wrote a book against the Gnostic heresies, which is extant in a Latin translation, and of which some fragments are preserved in the original Greek. There is no doubt that he knew the Fourth Gospel and treated it as being on the same level of authority as the other three. He ascribed it to a writer whom he calls either simply John, or John the disciple of the Lord. This John, he tells us, lived in Ephesus until the time of Trajan and was the teacher of Polycarp, whom he himself had known in his youth. Polycarp was Bishop of Smyrna and was put to death about A.D. 155. When called upon to deny Christ, he stated that he had served Him for eighty-six years. He therefore must have been born in A.D. 70, or even earlier. In any case he was a full-grown man when, according to tradition, John was living in Asia. The relevant passage in Irenæus is as follows : *

"And Polycarp was not only instructed in the faith by the Apostles and personally acquainted with many who had seen Christ, but he was also appointed by the Apostles for Asia as Bishop of the Church at Smyrna. Him even I saw in my early youth, for he remained a long time with us and was exceedingly old. . . . In the time of Anicetus, when staying at Rome, Polycarp converted many of these heretics to the Church of God, declaring that this was the one and only truth that he had received from the Apostles. Some also heard him say that John, the disciple of the Lord, went into the baths at Ephesus, but, seeing Cerinthus inside, he rushed away from the baths without bathing, and said : 'Let us fly, lest the baths fall, for Cerinthus the foe of truth is within.' The Church in Ephesus, founded by Paul, and where John lived unto the days of Trajan, is also a true witness of the traditions of the Apostles " (*Adv. Haer.* iii. 3, K. p. 125).

In his letter to Florinus, a friend who had fallen into heresy, quoted in Eusebius, *Hist.* v. 20 (K. p. 129), Irenæus writes as follows :

"For, when I was a boy, I saw thee in lower Asia

---

* Nearly all the passages pertinent to this inquiry will be found translated in Kidd's *Collection of Documents Illustrative of the History of the Church* (S.P.C.K.), or in Lightfoot's smaller edition of the *Apostolic Fathers*. These books will be referred to as K. and L., with the page where the extract is to be found.

with Polycarp moving in splendour in the royal court
and endeavouring to gain his approbation. I remember
the events of that time more clearly than those of
more recent years. For what boys learn, growing
with their mind, becomes joined to it : so that I am
able to describe the very place in which the blessed
Polycarp sat as he discoursed, and his goings out, and
his comings in, and the manner of his life, and his
physical appearance, and his discourses to the people,
and the accounts that he gave of his intercourse with
John and with the others that had seen the Lord.
And he remembered their words, and what he had
heard from them concerning the Lord and concerning
His miracles and teaching, having received them from
eyewitnesses of the life of the Word. Polycarp related
all things in harmony with the Scriptures.

"These things being told me by the mercy of God,
I listened to them attentively, noting them down, not
on paper, but in my heart. And continually through
God's grace I recall them faithfully."

Polycrates, who was Bishop of Ephesus in the last
decade of the second century, sent a letter to Victor
of Rome on the subject of the proper time at which
to observe Easter. This letter was a formal reply
written in the name of the bishops of Asia to a request
from the Bishop of Rome for information about the
usage of the various churches. This subject had also
been a matter of discussion between Polycarp and
Anicetus in the first half of the century when Polycarp
had refused to depart from the custom which he had
learnt from " John the disciple of the Lord and the
rest of the Apostles " (Eusebius, *H.E.* v. 24). Anicetus
not only allowed him to do what he thought right in
the matter, but also to celebrate in his church at Rome.
Polycarp must therefore have satisfied Anicetus as to
the Apostolic source of his custom, because Anicetus

would certainly have laid stress upon the Apostolic origin of the Roman Church and its traditions.

Polycrates states in his letter to Victor that he had been a Christian for sixty-five years, that seven of his relatives had been bishops, and that they and all the bishops who joined with him in sending the letter were agreed with regard to the time customary in Asia for keeping Easter.

He mentions John as follows: " Moreover, John, who was both a martyr (or witness) and a teacher, who reclined on the bosom of the Lord and, being a priest, wore the sacerdotal plate, fell asleep at Ephesus " (K. p. 136).

Tertullian and Clement of Alexandria, who both flourished during the last twenty years of the second century, refer to the presence of John in Asia quite incidentally, as if it were a fact that no one would think of disputing. Tertullian says: " For this is the manner in which the Apostolic churches transmit their registers, as the church of Smyrna which records that Polycarp was placed there by John, as also the church of Rome which makes Clement to have been ordained in like manner by Peter " (*De Præscript.* 32). In the thirty-sixth chapter of the same book he refers to John as " the Apostle."

Clement also refers to John as " the Apostle," and says that he lived at Ephesus (*Quis Dives*, 42, K. p. 163).

There seems to be no doubt that these two authors and Origen also regarded the " John," who was so familiar by name to the whole Christian Church as to need no other description than his mere name, as being the Apostle. They also unquestionably accepted the Fourth Gospel as of the highest authority and quoted it repeatedly.

Dionysius, Bishop of Alexandria, in the second half

of the third century undoubtedly regarded the Fourth Gospel as the work of the Apostle and believed that he died at Ephesus (Eusebius, *H.E.* vii. 25).

Dionysius was a pupil of Origen and had been head of the Catechetical School of Alexandria, which went back to Pantænus in the latter part of the second century.

Eusebius, the historian of the Church in the fourth century, never shows the slightest doubt that all the writers that he had consulted, many of whose works are now lost, believed that John the Apostle had ended his life in Asia in extreme old age.

Why, then, should doubt be thrown on a belief which seems so well attested ? Why should we not accept the references of Irenæus to " John the disciple of the Lord " as referring to the son of Zebedee, and thus settle the question of his residence in Asia once for all ?

The whole difficulty has arisen from the fragments of the writings of Papias which have been preserved by Eusebius and other writers.

Papias was Bishop of Hierapolis in Phrygia in the first half of the second century. He wrote a book called *The Exposition of the Oracles of the Lord.* According to Irenæus, he was a hearer of " John " and an associate of Polycarp (*Adv. Hær.* v. 33, L. p. 515),* and this statement is repeated by many subsequent writers, some of whom make it perfectly plain that by " John " they understood the son of Zebedee.

Thus Jerome (*Ep.* 75, 3) speaks of " Irenæus, a disciple of Papias, who was a hearer of John the Evangelist," and other later writers are quoted by Lightfoot to the same effect (L. pp. 520, 523, 524).

---

* In a fragment of Apollinarius, a successor of Papias as bishop of Hierapolis about A.D. 170, Papias is called "a disciple of John " (Lightfoot, *Apost. Fathers*, p. 523).

These authors are, of course, late and second or third hand ; but it must be remembered that some of them had access to the complete writings of Papias. It will be seen later what importance is attached to another statement which is attributed to Papias by other late authors. These statements should therefore be allowed to have some little weight.

In spite of all this, there is a difficulty in identifying the teacher of Papias with the Apostle, because it seems as if Papias did not claim to have personally known any of the Apostles.

Eusebius quotes a passage from the works of Papias to this effect :

"But I will not scruple also to give a place for you along with my interpretations to everything else that I learnt carefully and remembered carefully in time past from the Elders, guaranteeing its truth. . . . And, again, on any occasion when a person came in my way who had been a follower of the Elders, I would inquire about the discourses of the Elders—what Andrew, or Peter, or Philip, or Thomas, or James, or John, or Matthew, or any of the Lord's disciples said, and what Aristion and the Elder John, the disciples of the Lord, say " (Eusebius, *H.E.* iii. 39, K. p. 53).

Eusebius infers from this passage, first, that Papias by no means asserts that he was a hearer and eyewitness of the holy Apostles, but informs us that he received the doctrines of the Faith from their intimate friends ; secondly, that he refers to two persons called " John "—one whom he mentions with Peter and James and Matthew, evidently meaning the Evangelist, and another whom he names separately, and does not include in the number of the Apostles, because he places Aristion before him. This man he distinguishes by the name of " Elder."

He adds that Papias often mentions Aristion and

B

John the Elder by name, and gives their statements
in his works.

"So," says Eusebius, "it is here proved that the
statement of those is true who assert that there were
two of the same name in Asia and that there were also
two tombs at Ephesus, and that they are both called
John's until this day, which it is particularly necessary
to observe."

It is now very generally assumed, even by such
conservative critics as Lightfoot, that the view taken
by Eusebius is the correct one, namely, that Irenæus
was mistaken when he spoke of Papias as a hearer of
John the Apostle. It is also held that Eusebius was
justified in discovering a second John in this passage
among the persons from whom Papias says that he
got his information.

Much has been written on the subject, and those
who are interested can find the case against the
opinion of Eusebius stated in full in Salmon's *Introduction to the New Testament*, pp. 268 *sqq.*, and more
recently in Dr. Nolloth's *The Fourth Evangelist*, chap. v.

Until reading the last-named work the author of
this paper was halting between two opinions on this
question ; but after reading it he has come to the
conclusion that there is more to be said against the
opinion of Eusebius than for it.

First, it is to be observed that the interpretation
which Eusebius was the first to apply to this fragment
of Papias is the * only evidence that we have for the
existence of "John the Elder," who has become such
an important personage in modern criticism. All
later references to him are based on Eusebius ; before
Eusebius no one ever heard of him, as far as we know.

Eusebius quotes Dionysius of Alexandria in support
of his discovery of "John the Elder," but Dionysius

* Streeter, *Four Gospels*, p. 449.

never suggests that two Johns are to be found in Papias. The chapter in Eusebius which contains the opinions of Dionysius (*H.E.* vii. 25) is one which is well worth reading, as it shows how a bishop of the third century dealt with a critical question, and effectually disposes of the picture of the Fathers as credulous and uncritical writers, which seems to give plausibility to some modern theories.

Dionysius did not believe that the Gospel and Apocalypse were written by the same author. He was sure that the Gospel was written by the Apostle. By whom, then, was the Apocalypse written ?

By some one of the name of John evidently. Dionysius suggests that this unknown writer may have been one who was called after the Apostle, because of the love and admiration that he felt for him, just as, he says, many were called after Peter and Paul, as indeed we find to be the case in the earliest inscriptions in the Roman catacombs. He also mentions that he had heard that there were two tombs each bearing the name of John at Ephesus.

Now, Eusebius agreed with Dionysius that there were serious difficulties in attributing the Gospel and the Apocalypse to the same writer. He wanted to find a suitable author for the Apocalypse, and it is wonderful how the critical faculty is sharpened when a writer has a theory to support.

In his *Chronicle*, which was written before his *History*, he calls Papias " a hearer of John the Divine and Apostle," thus following the statement of Irenæus, who was surely likely to have known the facts. When he came to write his *History* he explained the relationship which existed between Papias and the Apostle in the way which we have seen above.

The whole question seems to turn on what Papias meant by the term " Elder." Before his time it had been used in the New Testament in several senses. In Heb. xi. 2, it is used of the Saints of the old covenant. It is used in many passages as the official designation of the higher order of ministers in the Christian Church.

It is used in 1 Peter iv. 1, by St. Peter of himself, as "fellow-elder" with other Christian ministers.

Papias plainly uses it as a synonym for Apostles. As will be seen by referring to the quotation on p. 7, he defines the "discourses of the Elders" as "what was said by Andrew, or by Peter, or by Philip, or by Thomas, or James, or John, or Matthew, or any other of the Lord's disciples." He then mentions two other "disciples"—Aristion and John; one of them he further distinguished by the title "Elder," the other he does not so distinguish.

Surely the obvious inference from this is that the John, who is mentioned last, belongs to the same class as Andrew, Peter and the others, while Aristion does not.

Papias is a clumsy writer; what he seems to wish to say is this : There was a time when he could get information about the sayings of many of the Apostles, such as those whom he mentions ; now these are dead, but one still survives, and he can still get information about what he says. Note the change of tense.

It has been urged that "Elder" was a technical term in Asia for those who had been followers of the Apostles, and there is no doubt that Irenæus used the word in this way. But this does not prove that Papias, who belonged to an earlier generation, must have used the term in this way also. To him the Apostles were plainly the "Elders," and we are not justified in taking the word in two different senses in the same passage.

Until 1862 the passages given above were the only

literary evidence available for or against the residence of the Apostle John in Asia, and nobody regarded it as doubtful, since the evidence of Irenæus seemed to be quite conclusive as to his presence there, whatever might be thought of the value of his testimony with regard to the authorship of the Fourth Gospel by the Apostle.

At that date a manuscript* of the *Chronicle* of Georgius Hamartolus, a Byzantine monk of the ninth century, was discovered, which differed from the manuscripts previously known in an important particular.

A few years later another manuscript was discovered which was thought by some to contain an epitome of the *History* of Philip of Side, an author who lived in the fifth century. This fragmentary manuscript contained a statement which seemed to confirm the statements contained in the manuscript of Georgius.

These two manuscripts contain a statement, made on the authority of Papias, that John the son of Zebedee was put to death by the Jews. This has been hailed as a great discovery in certain quarters, and is dignified with the name of the " Papias Tradition," and set up in opposition to the " Irenæus Tradition," or " Ephesian Legend," which it is believed to supersede.

The passages referred to above will be found in Lightfoot's *Apostolic Fathers*, pp. 518, 519, in the original Greek, and in Kidd, *op. cit.* pp. 267, 277. They should be carefully studied in the original.

Although these passages are referred to in many modern books and articles as settling the question of the authorship of the Fourth Gospel once for all, it is remarkable how seldom they are set out in full.

The last discovered fragment is, to use the words

* The Codex Coislinianus.

of Professor Ramsay, the work of a late epitomiser of
Philip of Side.

Dr. Nolloth, to whose work the writer owes some
of the details given above, will not allow that this
attribution is certain.

This Philip, to whom we may provisionally assign
the quotation, was an author of very little repute in
the opinion of Socrates (*Hist.* vii. 27) or of Photius
(*Cod.* 35). The latter says of him that his history
is full of undigested learning with very little bearing
on history at all, still less on Church history.

The words of the epitomiser of Philip are as
follows :

" Papias, Bishop of Hierapolis, who was a hearer
of John the Divine (ὁ θεολόγος) and a companion of
Polycarp, wrote five books of the Oracles of the Lord,
wherein giving a list of the Apostles, after Peter and
John, Philip and Thomas and Matthew, he included
among the disciples of the Lord, Aristion and a second
John, whom he called ' the Elder.' (He says) that
some think that this John is the author of the two
short and catholic Epistles which are published in the
name of John, and gives as a reason that the ancients
only accept the first Epistle. Some also have wrongly
considered the Apocalypse to be his. . . . Papias in
his second book says, that John the Divine and James
his brother were killed by the Jews." *

It is to be noted that this author begins by agreeing
with Irenæus that Papias was a hearer of John the
Divine, by which title there can be no doubt that he
means us to understand the Evangelist and Apostle.
He *may* have found this statement in Papias himself,
but it would not do to insist on this. There are many
other sources from which he might have drawn it, as
we have seen.

* See Appendix I.

Then he repeats the well-known passage from Papias, with which we have already dealt, and the explanation which Eusebius gives of it. If we could be sure that the next words were a quotation from Papias they would afford a proof that Papias considered that the Fourth Gospel, the First Epistle, and the Apocalypse were written by the Apostle, as it seems to make him attribute the Second and Third Epistles to the Elder. This would, however, be a very precarious argument.

Lastly, we come to the words on which the whole controversy is based. " Papias in his second book, says that John the Divine and James his brother were killed by the Jews."

Here we must notice first that the title " the Divine " cannot have come from Papias, as this title was only conferred on the Evangelist long after his time, and therefore the quotation cannot be verbally taken from Papias.

Secondly, we must notice that this last sentence flatly contradicts the first sentence, as Papias could not have been a disciple of John unless John had lived to be an old man, and, we might add, had come to Asia in his old age, for there is no probability that Papias went to Palestine.

The words of the manuscript of Georgius Hamartolus, discovered in 1862, are as follows :

" After Domitian, Nerva reigned one year, who recalled John from the island and allowed him to dwell in Ephesus. He was the sole survivor of the Twelve Apostles, and after writing his Gospel received the honour of martyrdom.* For Papias, Bishop of Hierapolis, who was an eyewitness of him, in the second book of the Oracles of the Lord says that he

* See Appendix II.

was killed by the Jews,* having, as is clear, with his brother fulfilled Christ's prophecy concerning them and their own confession and undertaking on His behalf. For when the Lord said to them, ' Are ye able to drink the cup that I drink of ? ' they readily assented and agreed. He said, ' My cup shall ye drink, and with the baptism that I am baptised shall ye be baptised.' And reasonably so, for it is impossible for God to lie. So, too, the learned Origen affirms in his interpretation of St. Matthew's Gospel that John was martyred, declaring that he had learnt the fact from the successors of the Apostles. And, indeed, the well-informed Eusebius also in his *Ecclesiastical History* says : ' Thomas received by lot Parthia, but John Asia, where he also made his residence and died at Ephesus.' "

It is really extraordinary that the slightest weight should be attached to this hopeless muddle which a stupid ninth-century compiler has made out of the statements of Papias, Irenæus, Eusebius, and Origen about John. If it were not for its precious confirmation of the "Papias Tradition," it would be treated as beneath contempt. Let it be noted, however, that this writer, who is presumed to have had all the works of Papias, confirms the tradition of the Church that John was the last survivor of the Twelve, that he was exiled to Patmos and returned to Ephesus, wrote his Gospel there and died at Ephesus.

If his testimony to the facts, in which he is supported by the almost unanimous consent of all other ecclesiastical writers, is not to be accepted, why should his testimony to the violent death of the Apostle at the hands of the Jews be accepted ?

There can only be one answer. Stupid people †

* On the suggestion of the Dean of Wells, I have taken the translation of these words from Bishop Lightfoot's *Essays on Supernatural Religion*, p. 211.

† Streeter, *The Four Gospels*, p. 435.

have their use. They blurt out awkward truths which wiser men keep silence about and suppress. The interpolator of Georgius and the epitomiser of Philip were too ignorant to see how, by unearthing this piece of information, they have upset all the careful arrangements by means of which the Fathers of the second century, by judicious forgetfulness and credulity, got the Fourth Gospel inserted into the Canon as the work of an Apostle.

Eusebius and Jerome were wiser; they saw how this statement of Papias contradicted the prevailing "Ephesian legend," and tacitly passed it over.

We are told by Dr. Moffatt and Dr. Charles that there were two traditions current in the Church of the second century, about the death of John. The one preserved by Papias—which was the true one—and the one preserved by Irenæus. It was considered of supreme importance that the Gospels should be provided with Apostolic authors. Therefore, the tradition of Irenæus was naturally preferred, because, if this was believed, it was possible to assign the Fourth Gospel (which was really the work of the Elder, or some one else) to the Apostle. Moffatt tells us (*Introduction to N.T.*, p. 616) that "Irenæus ignored the casual remark of Papias."

We are not told how the teachers and historians who "ignored" this awkward statement of Papias dealt with the inconvenient questions that might be put to them by other persons, who had read the works of Papias, and who were none too ready to accept the teaching of the Fourth Gospel.

It is too often tacitly assumed that the early Christian centuries were times of uncritical piety and sanctified ignorance. This supposition is quite incorrect. Many persons took up a critical attitude towards such books as were considered to be of doubtful

authenticity, such as the Second Epistle of Peter, the
Second and Third Epistles of John, the Apocalypse and
the Epistle to the Hebrews. The fact that the Gospel
was universally received as the work of the Apostle
John is not without significance in the present discussion. There seems to the writer to be no alternative between supposing that the epitomiser of
Philip and the interpolator of Georgius were mistaken
in their reading of Papias, or that Eusebius and
Jerome, not to mention Clement, Origen, Dionysius
and Irenæus, deliberately suppressed a piece of
information which they felt would be injurious to the
faith and traditions of the Church. Dr. Charles
assures us that : " No matter how valid the evidence
might be for the martyrdom of the Apostle before
A.D. 70, it could only be regarded as purely legendary,
seeing that, according to the most current view, John
the Apostle wrote the Apocalypse and wrote it in
Domitian's reign." He would therefore have us
believe that Irenæus, Tertullian and Origen " lost
all knowledge of the early martyrdom of John the son
of Zebedee " (*op. cit.* xxxvii.).

What probability there is in this suggestion we
must leave our readers to judge. To return to the
interpolator. It is obvious from the use of the connecting particle δηλαδή* that it was not Papias who
connected the supposed martyrdom of John with the
prophecy of Christ. Moffatt admits this. Apparently
it was the interpolator who made this connection, and
he does not seem very happy about it. He assures us
that it is a reasonable connection," for it is impossible
for God to lie," and then goes on to support his
statement by a reference to Origen. Fortunately
we have the passage in Origen to which he refers
in full.

* " As is clear."

In the *Homily* on Matthew xx. 23, in dealing with the words about the cup and the baptism, he says that many refer this saying to martyrdom, and that he agrees with them. This is, no doubt, what the interpolator is referring to.

Origen, however, goes on to say : " The sons of Zebedee did certainly drink the cup and were baptised with the baptism, since Herod killed James, the brother of John, with the sword, and the Emperor of the Romans, as tradition records, banished John to the Island of Patmos, for approving the word of truth with his testimony. John himself hands down in the Apocalypse in these words the circumstances of his martyrdom ($\mu\alpha\rho\tau\acute{\nu}\rho\iota\omicron\nu$), passing over the name of him by whom he was condemned. . . ."

Now, if we had not been able to check the way in which the interpolator understood, or rather misunderstood, Origen, we should have had an " Origen Tradition " about the violent death of the Apostle as well as a " Papias Tradition." Is it not at least possible that the interpolator may have misunderstood Papias, as he certainly misunderstood Origen ?

Then he makes confusion worse confounded by quoting Eusebius as a supporter of the story of the violent death of John, although all that Eusebius says is that he went to Ephesus and died there.

If, as we shall see later, the testimony of Irenæus to the presence of the Apostle in Asia is contemptuously dismissed on the ground that he makes mistakes and confusions in his other references to Apostles and their followers, what are we to say about the interpolator ?

This is all the really ancient evidence that can be produced in favour of the early and violent death of the Apostle John. It consists of a quotation from Papias made by two late and confused compilers, one of whom may have copied the other. In the case of both these writers, this statement is found in immediate connection with other statements which are quite inconsistent with it, when taken in the sense in which such critics as Schwartz and Wellhausen and their English followers take it.

Next, we must consider exactly what it is that this alleged quotation from Papias tells us.

It only tells us that John the son of Zebedee was put to death by the Jews. It does not tell us that he was put to death in Palestine, or that he was put to death early.

These additional and essential particulars were introduced into the story, as we shall see later, by certain modern critics on the slenderest grounds.

It cannot be too strongly insisted on that there is *absolutely no direct and early testimony* for these two details of the theory.

If the evidence of Papias is so valuable, what need is there that it should be embellished with these unauthorised additions ? Why has no one suggested that John may have been put to death in Asia by the Jews ? This would reconcile the statements of Irenæus and Papias, and not conflict very seriously with the traditions of the Church. Plainly because this solution of the difficulty does not get rid of any possible connection between the Apostle and the Fourth Gospel, which is the thing that is wanted.

The " Papias Tradition " seems, even in the opinion of its advocates, to need a good deal of extraneous support, and this is sought in many quarters. First we have the familiar and not very convincing argument from silence. Great importance is attached to the fact that no writer before A.D. 180 makes any mention of the presence of the Apostle in Asia.

We are told that neither Clement of Rome, Igna-

tius, Polycarp, Justin or Hegesippus makes any reference to his residence at Ephesus, and this is said to
be " very significant."

It is admitted that Clement had no occasion to
mention John ; but Ignatius was an eastern bishop
who wrote to the Church at Ephesus on his way to
Rome, and it is argued that, if he ever heard of the
presence of John there, he must have mentioned it.
" Paul," says Moffatt, " is the one Apostle mentioned (*Ad Eph.* xii. 2, Παύλου συμμύσται). The
description of the Ephesian Christians (*Eph.* xi. 2),
as οἱ καὶ τοῖς ἀποστόλοις πάντοτε συνήνεσαν ἐν δυνάμει
Ἰησοῦ Χριστοῦ, would be incredibly vague, if John
had occupied the local position which later tradition
assigned to him " (*op. cit.*, p. 614).

Charles says : " The reasonable inference from
the above silence is that Ignatius was not aware of
any residence of John the Apostle in Ephesus " (*op.
cit.* p. xlv.).

As usual, it is well to look at the context before
being quite so positive. Ignatius is praising the
Ephesians and comparing his condition as a condemned criminal with theirs. He says, " I know who
I am and to whom I write. I am condemned, you
have obtained mercy ; I am in danger, you are established in safety ; you are the passage for those who are
being slain for the sake of God, fellow-initiates with
Paul, who was sanctified, who gained a good report,
who was right blessed, in whose footsteps may I be
found when I shall attain unto God, who in every
Epistle makes mention of you in Christ Jesus "
(Kirsopp Lake's translation, p. 109).

Ignatius is here thinking of the Ephesians as his
kind helpers on his journey to martyrdom at Rome.
He remembers how St. Paul had also passed near them
and sent for their elders on the journey that led to

his arrest at Jerusalem, to his subsequent voyage to
Rome, and his death there. It is natural that he
should mention Paul, and Paul only, in such a context, especially if John had not also come to a violent
end. This interpretation not only seems to be the
obvious one, but it also has the support of Bishop
Lightfoot in his notes on the Epistles of St. Ignatius
(*Apostolic Fathers*, Ignatius, vol. i, p. 390).

As to the second passage quoted by Moffatt, it occurs
just before the one on which we have commented.
It is enough to point out that it refers to " Apostles." *
Paul was no doubt one : who were the others ? How
does this passage prove that John was not one of them ?

Why should it be " incredibly vague " to refer to
Paul and John as "Apostles " ?

If Polycarp does not mention the Apostle John
by name, he at any rate quotes the First Epistle of
John, which shows some familiarity with the " Johannine literature."

Justin mentions the Apocalypse by name, and
refers it to " John, one of the Apostles of Christ "
(*Dialogue with Trypho*, 81).† This is, of course, not
a direct reference to the presence of John in Asia,
but it is not complete silence, and should not be
treated as such. Dr. Charles makes no reference to
these words of Justin when he is treating of the
" silence " of the writers of the second century (*op.
cit.* p. xlv.), but on p. xxxvii. he has this curious note :
" Justin Martyr believes in the Apostolic authorship of the Apocalypse as early as A.D. 153 or there-
abouts. *A myth can arise in a very few years* : hence it

---

* Bousset thinks that John was probably one of these Apostles
(*Offenbarung*, p. 36).

† Harnack agrees that Justin regarded the Gospel as apostolic
and Johannine (*Chron. I.*, pp. 674, 683). Loisy also thinks that
Justin believed that the Apostle John lived in Asia (*Quatrième
Évangile*, p. 14).

is not strange that such writers as Hegesippus (*ob. cir.* 180), and subsequent writers such as Irenæus, Tertullian and Origen have lost all knowledge of the early martyrdom of the son of Zebedee."

Thus Dr. Charles himself confutes on one page the statement that he has made with such confidence on another. The " silence " of Justin is admitted not to be complete, and his one reference to John the Apostle is explained by the growth of " myth."

With this goes the significance of the " silence " of Polycarp, who must have known as much or as little as Justin, for Justin, we are told, lived in Ephesus for a time, and his evidence as to the authorship of the Apocalypse is felt to be so damaging to the " Papias Tradition " that the only way of meeting it is to suggest that " a myth can arise in a very few years."

What was the exact nature of this myth which is supposed to have arisen at Ephesus ? Apparently the sequence of events is imagined to have been something of this kind : John the Elder, who was regarded as a disciple of the Lord and as the greatest figure among the Christians in Asia both as an ecclesiastical ruler, a teacher and a writer, died somewhere between A.D. 100 and 110. In about twenty years a myth had grown up and thoroughly established itself, according to which John, the son of Zebedee, had come to Ephesus and filled there the place which had really been occupied by John the Elder. It was further believed that he had written the books which the Elder or his school had really written.

First, the Apocalypse was attributed to him, as is shown by the words of Justin ; then the Gospel and Epistle were attributed to him.

All this happened, because the need for an apos-

tolic author for the Fourth Gospel was felt to be so
urgent in order to resist the attacks of heretics on
the traditional faith and because of the peculiar
mentality of the time, that any story which contradicted this supposed necessity was " regarded as
legendary," no matter how valid the written or traditional evidence might be for its truth.

This took place while Polycarp was in his prime,
and he and his contemporaries apparently passed on
this " myth " in all good faith to Irenæus, who accordingly " lost all knowledge of the early martyrdom of
the son of Zebedee."

Irenæus in his turn founded the " Irenæus Tradition " which has misled historians ever since.   All
this is supposed to have taken place, not in an ignorant
and rural community, but in one of the greatest and
most highly educated centres of population in the
Græco-Roman world.

The man, whose memory is supposed to have
utterly perished from this civilised community, is one
who was, but twenty years before, so well known that
it was sufficient for him to designate himself in his
writings as " The Elder."

He had produced either personally or by his in-
spiring teaching two of the most remarkable and influential books that have ever been written, in the
admission of the critics themselves.   Yet all his friends
and disciples forgot him, and allowed his works to
be attributed to a man whom they had never seen
and who had been in his grave for sixty years in a far
distant land.   They either made up or received without examination a story that this man had come to
Ephesus and died there in extreme old age, and all
because he was one of the Twelve Apostles and
happened to have the same name as the great " Elder "
of Ephesus.

The only memorial of the " Elder " that remained was a cryptic reference in the works of a bishop of Hierapolis, a place of no special importance, about 100 miles from Ephesus. This reference was so obscure that it was not until 200 years afterwards that an ingenious historian interpreted it properly and restored at least the name of the " Elder " to the notice of Christendom, although he never recovered the credit that was due to him for his writings until our own times.

All this elaborate tissue of improbabilities has to be woven in order that the credit of the " Papias Tradition " and that of those modern writers that accept it may be safeguarded.

As for the " silence " of Hegesippus, Dr. Charles mentions it on one page without comment or explanation, as if it was discoverable from an exhaustive examination of his works. As a matter of fact we do not possess his works, and his " silence " is inferred from the fact that Eusebius does not happen to quote anything from him with regard to John. In his note on p. xxxvii, Dr. Charles says that Hegesippus had " lost all knowledge of the early martyrdom of John." He gives no reference, and we cannot tell what he is referring to. He seems to mean that Hegesippus did give some testimony to the prevailing belief that John the Apostle had been in Asia, otherwise how can it be known that he " lost all knowledge of his early martyrdom ? " If this is a correct interpretation of his meaning, what becomes of his statement as to the " silence " of second-century writers on p. xlv. ?

This exhausts all that can be brought forward from the evidence of the words or silence of ancient authors in favour of the " Papias Tradition." We now proceed to re-examine the " Irenæus Tradition." The question resolves itself into what Paley would have

c

called "a contest of opposite improbabilities"—the improbabilities that either Papias may have been mistaken or misquoted, or that Irenæus may have been mistaken. We have seen that it is not very improbable that Papias may have been misquoted : as to the probability of his being mistaken, if he ever made such a statement, we cannot speak with certainty. We can only say that Eusebius regarded him as a person of small intelligence, and that the only long passage that we possess of his works is singularly lacking in clearness, so much so that scholars of the greatest distinction are not yet agreed as to its meaning.

In considering the evidence of Irenæus, it is most important to keep in mind that we are *not* now discussing whether Irenæus was right when he attributed the Fourth Gospel to the Apostle John ; but whether he was right in supposing that the "John" about whom Polycarp spoke was the Apostle and not the Elder.

It is submitted that it would be easier for him to make a mistake by misunderstanding what Polycarp said to him about the first of these two questions than it would be for him to make a mistake about the second.

Attempts have been made to invalidate the evidence of Irenæus in three ways. First, it has been said that Irenæus was too young when he knew Polycarp to have retained any clear recollection of what he said about John. Secondly, it has been urged that he is such a careless writer that his testimony is not of much value in any case. Thirdly, a new theory has recently been brought forward according to which Irenæus, when he referred to "John," or "John the Disciple of the Lord," never meant to refer to the Apostle, but only to the Elder.

(1) Irenæus was born about A.D. 140. If Polycarp

was put to death in 155, Irenæus would be about fifteen when he last saw him. In view, however, of his solemn asseveration of the clearness of his recollection of those early days and of the soundness of the principle which he lays down that " what boys learn, growing with their mind, becomes joined to it," we cannot in fairness say that he was too young, or too inattentive to have retained a correct recollection of what Polycarp told him about John. A Christian boy must have been well aware, even at the age of fourteen, that his faith put him in danger of losing his life, and therefore he would be keenly interested in anything that had any bearing on its evidences or reliability.

It has been urged with a certain amount of plausibility that Irenæus was so young that he might have misunderstood the witness of Polycarp as to the *authorship* of the Fourth Gospel : that he might have understood Polycarp to have said that it was actually written by John the Apostle, when the fact was that it was founded on the recollections of John, and put in its present form by the Elder, or some other member of John's school of thought.

This might be possible in the case of a boy, supposing that he had never met any one in later life who could have given him more correct information— which is obviously absurd—and supposing that John the Apostle had actually been in Asia. The situation which the modern theory presupposes is quite different to this. It is now supposed that when Irenæus was a boy and the Canon was in course of formation, it was felt to be of the first importance to provide as many books of the New Testament as possible with apostolic authors, since to be written by an Apostle was an almost essential qualification for any book which was to be recognised as canonical. Therefore, Irenæus,

boy as he was, may well have often heard discussions
about the authorship of the Fourth Gospel and been
deeply interested in them, as intelligent boys often
are in matters that interest their elders. The modern
theory also presupposes that John the Apostle had
never been in Asia, and that judging from their " very
significant " silence, Polycarp, Justin, and Ignatius
knew this quite well—that is, unless we accept
Dr. Charles' myth theory.

Everybody in Asia whom Irenæus met with in
his youth must have known the facts also, so that
Irenæus was by no means dependent on Polycarp for
this piece of information.

As may be seen by a reference to p. 4, the information that Irenæus owed to Polycarp had to do,
not merely with the fact that John the Apostle had
been in Asia, but with something far more intimate.

What he got from Polycarp were those personal
anecdotes, which old men can alone impart and which
young men often value so highly.

We have, however, already seen that the " silence "
of Justin and Polycarp is not absolute and that Dr.
Charles is compelled to admit that even in A.D. 135,
five years before the birth of Irenæus, it was believed in Ephesus that John the Apostle had written
the Apocalypse.

This admission, which seems to be inevitable,
renders it improbable in the highest degree that
Irenæus can have misunderstood Polycarp. Polycarp
himself must have been mistaken or must have
deceived his hearers. He must have had some
interest in the question, since he quotes the First
Epistle of John.

Harnack does not shrink from this explanation of
the difficulty. In his *Chronologie*, I. pp. 678, 679, as
quoted by Sanday, *Criticism of the Fourth Gospel*,

p. 63, he says : " Papias, through the oral traditions about which he took so much trouble, already stood under the influence of presbyters of whom some, *perhaps purposely*, started the legend that the Presbyter was the Apostle." And again he speaks of " the legend *purposely set on foot* that the author of the Gospel was the son of Zebedee."

It is well to see to what the theories we have been discussing naturally lead, in the opinion of so distinguished an advocate of the " Presbyter John " theory, although it is fair to add that Dr. Harnack is a determined opponent of the theory that John the son of Zebedee died in Palestine as a martyr. Are we, then, still willing to do what the earlier and cruder opponents of Christianity did : to charge the men of the first or second generation of Christians with forgery and fraud, especially when there was so very little motive for such conduct, as there must have been, supposing that the " Elder " was a real person, and had all the qualifications for a suitable Evangelist with which modern criticism endows him ?

We must also remember that it was just as difficult in the first century, as it is now, " to bring a clean thing out of an unclean." And it may be well to quote here the words with which Dr. Sanday closes his book on the Fourth Gospel : " A view of history that cannot be expressed in terms fit to describe the operations of Divine Providence ; that sees in it nothing but high blunders and gross deteriorations ; that regards the Church of Christ as built on fundamental untruth, which only becomes worse and not better as the centuries advance ; such a view seems to me to be not loyal and not really Christian."

(2) The second objection made to the testimony of Irenæus is that he is a careless writer, and has made other similar confusions in his writings.

We are told that he confuses James the brother of the Lord with James the son of Zebedee, and makes the latter preside at the Council of Jerusalem (*Adv. Hær.* iii. 12). (Charles, *op. cit.* p. xlix.; Moffatt, *op. cit.* p. 609.)

When a statement like this is made by an author who has a reputation for scholarship, the ordinary reader is generally content to accept it and to pass on, especially when the source of the quotation is rather inaccessible.

Let us, however, examine this allegation for ourselves and see whether it is just or not.

The section in question contains an account of the Apostolic preaching mostly in the very words of the *Acts*, with a few comments by the author. In the course of this account he mentions the Council of Jerusalem, just as any modern writer might do, and mentions the part that James took in it. He says not one word that could make any one think that by this James he meant any one but the brother of the Lord. In the last section of the chapter we get these words : " The Apostles who were with James allowed the Gentiles to act freely, committing us to the Spirit of God; but they themselves, knowing the same God, continued in their former observances, so that Peter also, fearing that he should be blamed by them—although, because of his vision and because of the Spirit which had rested upon them, he had at first eaten with the Gentiles—when certain came from James, separated himself and did not eat with them. Paul said that Barnabas did the like. So, then, Apostles, whom the Lord made witnesses of His whole life and teaching (for Peter, James and John are found everywhere present with Him) behaved with reverence towards the dispensation of the law which is according to Moses, setting forth that it came from one and the

same God.   As we have already shown, they would
not have done this, if they had learnt from the Lord
that there was another Father besides Him who made
the dispensation of the law."

Is it fair to infer from this that Irenæus confused
James the brother of the Lord with James the son of
Zebedee ?

Would such an inference have been made by any
one who had not a thesis to support, that was badly
in need of any and every support for it that he could
find ?

Surely a man who knew the Acts of the Apostles
as well as Irenæus did, cannot have made such a mistake, and should not be charged with it, unless he makes
it unmistakably.   Here he is obviously using the
word " Apostles " rhetorically, and must have intended
to refer to Peter alone, or to Peter and John.

This is quite a fair example of the usual " critical "
handling of ancient authors, who are alternately
treated as fools or oracles, according as they do, or
do not, speak as the fashionable theory of the day
demands.

In the next place it is said that he also confuses
Peter and Jesus, as if Acts v. 15 applied to the
latter.

The passage in which this supposed confusion
takes place is in the newly discovered *Apostolic
Preaching*, chapter 71.

We may have to grant that there is some careless-
ness or confusion here ; but it is also possible that
Irenæus may be referring to some forgotten tradition
of the miracles of Christ.   The worst charge that can
be brought against Irenæus is the well-known one that
in *Adv. Hær.* ii. 22, he infers either from the Fourth
Gospel (ii. 20, viii. 57), or from the Asiatic presbyters,
who claimed to hand on John's tradition, that Jesus

did not die until the reign of Claudius (Moffatt, *op. cit.* p. 609).

This certainly seems a strange error. Moffatt asserts that this fantastic inference, drawn from the Johannine literature, could never have come from a disciple who was one of the Twelve, and, as Irenæus says that the elders bore witness that John had handed down this tradition to them, he concludes that this is an additional proof that the Apostle never was in Asia.

This strange tradition, if regarded in this way, would be equally valid as a proof that the " Elder," in whose existence so many of the critics believe, never was in Asia either, or, that if he was, he knew very little about the life of Christ or the Synoptic Gospels. If the works of Irenæus had come down to us in small fragments, and the passage mentioned above had been one of them, it is certain that it would have been used to prove that he " knew nothing " of our Gospels. How absurd this inference would have been we only know because we possess so large a portion of his works.

How he came to have got hold of this tradition must remain unexplained in the present condition of our knowledge, but the fact that he did get hold of it and believe it does not prove that John never was in Asia, unless it also proves that Irenæus did not know our Gospels.

Lastly, Irenæus is charged by Dr. Charles (*op. cit.* p. xlix.) with the serious error of calling one of his authorities in one place " a disciple of the Apostles " and in another place " a disciple of a disciple of the Apostles " (*Adv. Hær.* iv. 27, 32).

We are also gravely assured that, since Polycrates, Clement of Alexandria, Tertullian and Eusebius confused Philip the Evangelist with Philip the Apostle, therefore Irenæus *may* have confused John the Apostle with John the Elder.

Of course he *may* have done so : but is there anything more than the lowest of probabilities in the argument that because one set of men confused two persons who lived long before their time and in whom they had no special interest, therefore another man may have confused two other persons in whom he had a good reason to be interested, especially when, as is the case here, it is not proved whether one of these latter two persons ever existed ?

Supposing we grant for the sake of argument that Irenæus did make certain mistakes in his writings— we have seen what kind of errors are charged against him—are his alleged mistakes the same in kind as his mistake would have been if he had confused together two such well-known figures as John the Elder and John the Apostle, supposing that John the Apostle had never been in Asia ?

Moffatt tells us (*op. cit.* p. 616) that "Irenæus ignored the casual remark of Papias," as if Papias was the only person from whom he could have heard of the death of John the Apostle. It has never been explained how it was that Papias, and apparently Papias alone, knew the truth about this matter.

In another place in the same book (p. 609), he says that the memory of Irenæus "misled him here, as elsewhere, partly owing to his desire to safeguard the apostolic origin of the Fourth Gospel."

This is unreasonable. A man's memory does not mislead him, when he has a purpose in view, in making a statement over and over again about a question of this importance, even though that purpose be the safeguarding of a pious fraud.

One can only apply to such critical methods the words of Dr. Sanday, "That is another of the methods of modern criticism that seem to me sorely in need of reforming. I hope that a time may come when it will be considered as wrong to libel the dead as it is to libel the living" (*Criticism of the Fourth Gospel*, p. 81).

Many of the theories of the present day with regard to the events of the second century depend on the unproved hypothesis that, while the Canon of Scripture was being formed, every effort was made to find apostolic authors for writings which were candidates for admission into the sacred circle. This hypothesis leaves quite unexplained the fact that two of the Gospels then admitted into the Canon were not the work of Apostles, or even of eyewitnesses of the life of Christ.

Justin is quite content to state that the Gospels were written by the Apostles * and those that followed them, and Tertullian says, " Denique nobis fidem ex Apostolis Johannes et Matthæus insinuant, ex Apostolicis [that is, ' of the followers of the Apostles '] Lucas et Marcus instaurant " (*Adv. Marc.* iv. 2).†

There was no pressing reason why the truth should have been concealed by a conveniently forgetful memory when " John the Elder " would have been quite as satisfactory an Evangelist as Mark or Luke, and perhaps more so.

Moreover, if it had been necessary to make this convenient exercise of memory in order to obtain or safeguard canonicity for the Fourth Gospel, why did not Irenaeus make a formal statement that the Gospel was written by the Apostle John ?

As it is, he refers to the connection between John and the Gospel so casually, and treats it so entirely as a matter about which there was no dispute, that it has been, and still is, disputed whether he may be counted

* Dialogue 103.   † I owe this quotation to Dr. Nolloth.

as a witness to the Apostolic authorship of the Gospel at all.

Lastly, what confusion it would introduce into all historical investigation, if we were to lay down as a canon of criticism, that no writer is to be believed in any of his statements, because he has made a mistake, or even several mistakes, in other parts of his writings about quite other matters.   We should rather ask what probability there is that he observed some things with more attention than others, or what opportunity he had of being better informed of some things than of others, before we infer from one or two demonstrated mistakes that any of his other statements must be incorrect.   Now, we have seen that Irenæus affirms in the most solemn way that he remembered the details of his intercourse with Polycarp and the latter's reminiscences about John particularly well.   And yet we are not to believe him on this particular question, because, forsooth, he may have confused James the son of Zebedee with James the brother of the Lord, in whom he had no reason to have any special interest.

This is simply a question of common sense.   No special learning or critical acumen will be any particular help in deciding such a problem, which is decided by considering the probable way in which a man's memory will act.

We can only judge of such things from the way in which men generally act and from our own experience.

The writer may perhaps be allowed to introduce a rough parallel from his own recollections.   When he was a boy, his father used to talk to him about his old schoolmaster, and he distinctly remembers a day when his father brought home a Latin dictionary which he had bought, because it was the work of that old schoolmaster. Supposing that the writer has made certain slips in his writings, would that invalidate his testimony to the fact that a certain person had been his father's schoolmaster, or even to the fact that his father had told him that this schoolmaster had written a certain dictionary which he used to possess ? And yet the life of the writer is in no danger because of his faith in such a statement. The life of Irenæus was : he had seen the terrible persecution at Vienne, and sat in the seat of a martyr bishop.

Such things sharpen the memory about essential points of evidence and do not leave much room for intentional forgetfulness.

(3) The difficulty of believing that Irenæus could have confused the two Johns is so great that a new theory has recently been brought forward according to which he never intended to refer to John the Apostle at all.*

Dr. Burney in his *Aramaic Origin of the Fourth Gospel* argues on linguistic and other internal evidence that the Gospel was written in Aramaic, possibly in Antioch by some follower of our Lord, who was well acquainted with the teaching of the Rabbinic schools and with the Hebrew Old Testament.

He believes that this disciple cannot have been John the son of Zebedee, because he regards it as improbable that he could have had the training necessary for the production of such a book, especially as we are told that, when Peter and John were brought before the Rulers of the Jews, they appeared to them unlearned and ignorant men.

He accepts without examination the story of the early death of the son of Zebedee as told by Philip and Georgius, and goes on to suppose that all the references in the Gospel to the disciple whom Jesus loved do not refer to him at all. This disciple was a young man of Jerusalem of priestly family who was

* By Hugo Delff.

well educated in Rabbinic learning and who was therefore able to understand the discourses of our Lord in Jerusalem as none of the rude Galilean fishermen could have done. He was present at the last supper and lay on the breast of the Lord and stood beside His Cross. He was one of the two unnamed disciples mentioned in the account of the last meeting by the sea of Galilee in the last chapter of the Gospel. He afterwards went to Antioch where he wrote the Gospel in Aramaic, and he spent his latter days at Ephesus where he was known as John the Elder. This is the man that Irenæus refers to when he speaks of John, or John the disciple of the Lord.

This explanation clears the memory of Irenæus from the charge of confusing the John who lived in Ephesus with the Apostle. It explains the reference of Polycrates to this John as a priest who wore the sacerdotal plate, and it provides the Gospel with an author who is in every way most satisfactory, as not only an eyewitness, but an intelligent and educated eyewitness. This is a very attractive theory; it clears up certain difficulties which have always been felt with regard to the Johannine problem.

This theory rests on two bases : first, the alleged improbability that the son of Zebedee could have the training which would have enabled him to understand and report our Lord's discourses, and, second, the alleged fact that Irenæus never calls the John that he refers to an Apostle.

As to the first, we really know too little about the circumstances of the household of Zebedee and the capacities of his sons to be absolutely certain about this. Even if the Rulers of Jerusalem professed to see in Peter and John only unlearned and ignorant men, this did not prevent even them from marvelling at their eloquence and taking knowledge of them that they had been with Jesus. When we know neither what the natural capacity of the son of Zebedee was, nor the education that he received, nor the effect that contact with Christ may have had on him, not to mention the results of the inspiration of the Spirit, it is rather presumptuous to assume out of hand that he cannot possibly have had the requisite gifts and training which would have enabled him to write the Fourth Gospel.

As for the second point, we are told that Irenæus calls the man whom he supposed to have written the Gospel, " John the disciple of the Lord," fourteen times, and " John " thirty-one times, and the "Apostle" only twice, and then he speaks of him as " the Apostle " after he has called him simply " John " (*op. cit.* p. 139).

He never calls him the Apostle John, and, when he describes the authors of the Gospels, he calls them Matthew the Apostle, Mark the interpreter and follower of Peter, Luke the follower and disciple of the Apostles, and John the disciple of the Lord (*Adv. Hær.* iii. 9, 10, 11).

Matthew is called the Apostle once, Peter once, Paul ninety-two times.

This is supposed to prove that Irenæus did not regard the John that he speaks about as being one of the number of the Twelve.

It is admitted that he is virtually called " the Apostle " twice, and is several times equated with the Apostles in such phrases as " John and the other Apostles." *

This is the evidence that satisfies Dr. Burney that there was only one John in Ephesus, and he was the person whom Papias calls " the Elder," and Irenæus " John the disciple of the Lord."

What would seem to follow from Dr. Burney's

---

* *Adv. Hær.* ii. 22–25 ; iii. 3, 4, 21–23.

table is rather that Irenæus preferred not to refer to members of the Twelve as Apostles. He called them much more frequently by their names alone. The title Apostle he seems to have principally kept for Paul, who was not one of the number of the Twelve.

Moreover, Irenæus does not confine his use of the term Apostle to those to whom it is applied in the Gospels and Acts. He calls John the Baptist an Apostle in *Adv. Hær.* iii. 9, 4.

To suppose that the fact that Irenæus never called the author of the Fourth Gospel John the Apostle proves that he could not have been one of the Twelve seems rather a bold conclusion to draw from such a premise.

The main objection to the theory is this. It does not in any way account for the belief that undoubtedly soon sprung up that John the Apostle had been in Asia. It clears Irenæus from the blame of this mistake ; but it transfers the blame of it to Tertullian, Clement of Alexandria, Origen and Dionysius, who certainly believed, as we have shown that the John who lived in Asia and wrote the Gospel, was the Apostle.

It will perhaps be granted that Tertullian, who was a contemporary of Irenæus and was acquainted with Greek and knew the works of Irenæus—as appears from his treatise against the Valentinians, chapter five, where he calls him, " Irenæus the very exact inquirer into all doctrines "—would be as likely to have understood to whom Irenæus was referring, when he wrote of " John the disciple of the Lord," as any Oxford professor of the present century.

Now, in his book *De præscriptione hæreticorum* we read this (chap. xxii.) : " Was anything again concealed from John, the Lord's most beloved disciple, who used to lean on His breast, to whom alone the Lord pointed

out Judas as the traitor and whom He commended to
Mary as a son in His own stead ? Of what could He
have meant those to be ignorant, to whom He even
exhibited His own glory with Moses and Elias, and the
Father's voice moreover from heaven ? "

Nothing can be plainer than this. Tertullian
identifies the Beloved Disciple, the unnamed watcher
at the Cross of Christ, who claims to have written the
Gospel, with the son of Zebedee in the most unequivocal
way.

Dr. Burney's theory also contradicts the theory,
to which we have already referred, that all the
authorities of the Church in the second century were
desperately anxious at all costs, even at the cost of
fraud, according to Harnack (see p. 27), to find an
apostolic author for the Fourth Gospel.

Irenæus was obviously, if this theory be true, not
conscious of any such pressing anxiety in this matter
as would make him either allow "his memory to mislead
him," or cause him to regard the evidence for the
martyrdom of John the son of Zebedee as " purely
legendary, no matter how valid it might be."

So these theories devour one another, although they
are all intended to accomplish the great and supremely
important end of depriving the Fourth Gospel of an
apostolic author, against the plainest witness of
antiquity.

Let us, however, suppose, for the sake of argument,
that Dr. Burney's theory is true, and that Irenæus
never meant to attribute the Gospel to the Apostle.
How did Tertullian, in that case, come to make the
mistake which he did make ? Moreover, although
Irenæus was born in the East, he spent much of his
life as a bishop in the West, and his knowledge that
the son of Zebedee had nothing to do with the Gospel
must have gone with him to Gaul. What became

of it there? Lastly, how did Justin, who had been in Ephesus before Irenæus was born, come to ascribe the Apocalypse to the Apostle?

Dr. Burney does not say one word about the way in which these facts are to be accounted for. All he does is to say that when Eusebius read the passage in Papias about the two Johns he "jumped to the conclusion" that John the Apostle mentioned in the list must be the Evangelist (*op. cit.* p. 141).

Surely he cannot mean that he attributes the beginning of the mistake to Eusebius. What else could Eusebius possibly do? The prevalent opinion in his time was undoubtedly that the Apostle had died in Asia and written the Gospel there. He was not acute enough to see that he and all other Church writers had quite misunderstood the meaning of Irenæus when he referred to John the disciple of the Lord and meant thereby not the Apostle, but the Elder!

Then what necessity is there for this theory? Scarcely any—unless we agree with Dr. Burney that it is proved beyond the shadow of a doubt that John the son of Zebedee could not have written the Fourth Gospel, because he was not well enough educated. *Entia non sunt multiplicanda præter necessitatem.*

We now pass on to examine the words of Christ in the twentieth chapter of Matthew and the tenth chapter of Mark, where He promises that James and John shall drink His cup and be baptised with His baptism.

We are told that, unless we are prepared to admit that this prophecy of Jesus was not fulfilled, we are bound to allow that the two brothers must have suffered a "martyrdom of death," and also *that this must have come to pass by the time Mark's Gospel was published* (Moffatt, *op. cit.* p. 603).

D

The original father of the theory, Schwartz, went much further. He says : "If one deals seriously with the demand of the sons of Zebedee for the two places of honour on the right and left of the returning Messiah, then it is not merely impossible to avoid the conclusion that they both died as martyrs, but the sitting on both sides is only comprehensible and clear, if in point of fact they left the earth at the same time and together. Finally, I do not know how the whole claim could have been framed if they were not the first, and did not for a considerable time remain the only ones who took up their cross." This is exquisite. It quite omits to notice that the sons of Zebedee were never promised the two seats that they asked for. Of course Schwartz considers it self-evident that the saying of Jesus is not authentic, but a *vaticinium post eventum* attributed to Jesus, which could not possibly have been put in His mouth, unless it was known that the event to which it is supposed to refer had actually occurred.

It is only on this basis that the passage can have any value as a piece of historical proof of the martyrdom of John to those who do not believe in the supernatural foresight of Jesus, and this should be particularly observed.

Schwartz, "with the *naïveté* of a philologist and without any attempt at proof," as Zahn says, goes on to assume, in order to remove obstacles to his theory of the simultaneous martyrdom of the sons of Zebedee, that the author of *Acts* " for the sake of the dominant Ephesian legend" omitted the name of John in chapter xii. 2, where the death of James is recorded, and he supposes that the John mentioned as one of the pillars of the Church in Jerusalem in Gal. ii. 9, is John Mark, who is not to be identified with the Mark of Col. iv. 10.

It is only fair to say that the more sober English critics cannot quite follow Schwartz in every detail of his theory, but they try to retain the part that they consider least open to fatal objections, namely, that John was put to death in Palestine, not with James, but at any rate before the Gospel of Mark was put into writing.

Now, it should be observed on what supposition this last part of the theory must rest. It either rests on the supposition of Schwartz that the words of Christ are not genuine, but a *vaticinium post eventum*, put into His mouth, and that the whole story is invented to afford a setting for them, or else it rests on the supposition that, allowing the words and the incident to be genuine, they would never have been inserted in the Gospel or allowed to stand there unless they had found their fulfilment exactly in the way the critics consider necessary. It cannot be too clearly understood that it is on this basis *alone* that any support can be found for that part of the theory that regards the death of John as having taken place before the Synoptic Gospels were written.

Those who approve of this absolutely subjective method of New Testament criticism, which treats the Evangelists as at best cunning or credulous manipulators of tradition, or at worst shameless falsifiers always working with an eye to some ulterior purpose, may find some force in this argument, if they please ; but it should not be accepted as the last word in historical criticism by persons who do not share these views, without a clear understanding of the fact that this theory does not rest on historic evidence at all, but only upon a theory of the way in which the books of the New Testament were compiled, with which they do not agree.

Let us, however, suppose that Christ did really

speak these words, that He had supernatural insight into the future, and that they were written down in the Gospels before the death of John. Does it follow that they were never fulfilled, and that Christ was a false prophet ?

We are told that it is evident from such passages as Mark xiv. 36, that the drinking of the cup must mean violent death, and that " the hypothesis that Jesus was simply referring in general terms to persecution and hardship, does not do justice to the specific and definite character of the prediction " (Moffatt, *op. cit.* p. 602).*

It is certainly very strange that until this passage was wanted as a support to the Papias Tradition about the early death of John, this inevitable explanation was never heard of except in a rhetorical passage in one of Chrysostom's orations and in the passage quoted from " Georgius " above. It was his interpolator who directed the attention of the critics to the passage, and then the scales fell from their eyes and they saw its meaning plainly for the first time.

It is unreasonable to speak of a man who had been banished to the mines in the Island of Patmos as only having to undergo " persecution and hardship." Such a sentence was intended to be a condemnation to a slow and lingering death, and was frequently spoken of as martyrdom by Church writers. (*See* Ramsay, *First Christian Century*, p. 43.) Our Lord often spoke in figures, and it would be as absurd to tie this passage down to this one meaning, as it would be to say that no one can be His disciple unless he goes about his work literally carrying a cross.

One has only to think of the language in which He prophesied the destruction of Jerusalem and the end of the world to see what strange results would be pro-

* See Appendix III.

duced if this very modern method of interpretation was applied to all His words.

If New Testament authority is to be appealed to, we think that the twenty-first chapter of the Fourth Gospel should not be passed over.

Putting the matter at the lowest, the Fourth Gospel (whoever wrote it) was in existence at the time of Papias and deserves some recognition as reflecting beliefs current at the time when it was written. Let us, for the sake of argument, accept the position that this chapter was not part of the original Gospel, but was written with the object of making the Church believe that the Gospel was written by the Apostle John.

In this object it undoubtedly succeeded. Now, if it was well known in the Church that John the son of Zebedee had been put to death early and so fulfilled the (*ex hypothesi*) forged prophecy of his death put into the mouth of Christ, why did the author of this further forgery go out of his way to make Christ prophesy that he would live a long time ?

The tradition that John the Apostle lived to a great age must have arisen very early, or else why should this obscure saying about his tarrying until Christ should come have been inserted into this " tendenz-schrift " which was intended, as Professor Bacon assures us, to make the Church of Rome accept the Gospel as of apostolic authority, and to rehabilitate Peter, who had not been treated with sufficient respect in the earlier part of the Gospel ? Evidently the Church of Rome " knew nothing " of the early death of the Apostle.

Moreover, if we are to believe Schwartz that the writer of *Acts* omitted any reference to the simul-taneous execution of James and John " for the sake of the dominant Ephesian legend," we shall have to place the rise of the "Ephesian legend" very early. What then becomes of Dr. Burney's theory and of the "significant silence" of all second-century writers about the presence of the Apostle in Asia, if the "Ephesian legend" held the field so thoroughly when *Acts* was written that the writer or redactor had to doctor his text to make it fit in with the current belief?

There is, we are told, a further piece of evidence to be noted. Let us give it in the words of Dr. Latimer Jackson in his book *The Problem of the Fourth Gospel*, p. 145 :

"To turn first to Clement of Alexandria. In the passage in question he appeals to Holy Scripture in its demands to risk martyrdom sooner than deny Christ ; he proceeds to quote Heracleon, who, says he, affirms that there are two ways of making confession ; he then instances Heracleon's allusion to some who had not sealed their faith with their lives : ἐξ ὧν Ματθαῖος, Φίλιππος, Θωμᾶς, Λευὶς καὶ ἄλλοι πολλοί. The distinction between Matthew and Levi, met with now and again elsewhere, is of no great moment. The one point to fasten on is the *explicit denial of red martyrdom* in a context from which the name of the Apostle John is absent—he is surely not relegated to the many others. Clement, it would appear, makes no demur. Is there much force in the suggestion that, if the Apostle's name is absent, sufficient explanation is forthcoming in stories already current as to the Patmos-exile and the cauldron of boiling oil ? "

The inference from this is obviously that Heracleon believed that John had suffered death by "red-martyrdom" and that Clement had nothing to say against it. Moffatt also assures us (*op. cit.* p. 606), that John's name is "significantly omitted from the list" and that it is "hardly possible that he could have been included among the many others, on account of his contemporary importance." On this we have several remarks to offer.

First, the evidence of Heracleon is not discounted, as that of Irenæus is, because he distinguishes between Matthew and Levi. This is " of no great moment " when it is found in an author whose evidence is believed to tell in favour of the " Papias Tradition." Second, John the Apostle suddenly becomes of considerable " contemporary importance " in the time of Heracleon, although elsewhere * we are encouraged to note that the place that he occupies in the rest of the New Testament is not really so great as to make it probable that he was the disciple whom Jesus loved.

Let us, however, refer to the passage in Clement, which is to be found in *Stromateis*, iv. 9.

Heracleon is speaking of the distinction that is to be made between those who confess Christ with their lives and those that confess Him with their voice. He goes on to say that some people think that confession made with the voice before a tribunal is the only true confession, but that they are mistaken in this, because hypocrites can confess with this confession.

Then he adds : " But neither will this utterance be found to be spoken universally, for all the saved have confessed with this confession made with the voice, and departed, of whom are Matthew, Philip, Thomas, Levi and many others."

There seems to be no intention on the part of Heracleon in this passage to make an exhaustive list of the Apostles who escaped " red martyrdom," and therefore it contains no proof whatever that John was put to death by violence. All it does is to include Matthew, Philip, Thomas and Levi among the saved

* By Dr. Burney.

who have made a good confession and departed—it is not said in what way—out of this life.

This argument is such an excellent example of the length to which some so-called historical critics will go in gathering evidence in support of an untenable theory, that it has been thought well to dwell on it at some length.

Clement of Alexandria, who is one of the witnesses quoted by Eusebius for the long residence of John in Asia, is brought forward as one in whose mind the true Papias Tradition still "vibrated," for he says in one place (*Strom.* vii. 17), that "The teaching of the Apostles, embracing the ministry of Paul, ends with Nero." In another he tells the story of a young man who became a robber and who was converted by the Apostle in Asia (*Quis dives*, 42).

Here, of course, the extract which accords with the "Papias Tradition" is accepted as unquestionably true and the other extract dismissed as a fabrication, "like the tale of Sir Walter Raleigh and his cloke" (Moffatt, p. 607).

The decision of the question obviously cannot be influenced much either way by these quotations which cancel each other, supposing that Clement meant his first statement to be taken literally.

Lastly, we are referred to the calendars or lists of the festivals of the martyrs that were observed in various churches

A Syriac martyrology, which is said to date from the fourth century, gives the following :

"The names of our lords the martyrs and victors and their days on which they gained their crowns :

Dec. 26th.—Stephen the Apostle, the head of the martyrs.

" 27th.—John and James, the Apostles at Jerusalem.

Dec. 28th.—In the town of Rome, Paul the Apostle and Simon Cephas, the head of the Apostles of the Lord."

About a hundred years later we have a Carthaginian martyrology which contains the following :

Dec. 25th.—The festival of our Lord Jesus Christ, the Son of God.
„ 26th.—The festival of Stephen the first martyr.
„ 27th.—The festival of St. John the Baptist and St. James the Apostle, whom Herod slew (*quem Herodes occidit*).
„ 28th.—The festival of the Infants whom Herod slew.

These entries in the martyrologies are taken as evidence of a belief deep down in the mind of the Church that John had met with a violent death.

Charles remarks that " seeing that the statements with regard to James, Paul and Peter are trustworthy, there appears no reason for questioning that concerning John" (*op. cit.* p. 49), a truly amazing piece of reasoning.

What if a Roman Catholic controversialist were to argue that because the statement about James in this martyrology was trustworthy it settled the much-disputed questions as to whether Peter was ever in Rome and was the head of the Apostles of the Lord ?

All that these calendars can prove is the existence in the fourth and fifth centuries of a belief that the days observed were connected with the death of the persons honoured on them. When a statement in a calendar of this date contradicts the universal belief not only of the days in which it was written, but also of two centuries previously, it seems very probable either that there is some mistake in our copy of the calendar, or in our understanding of it.

But this evidence is not good enough unless it is improved. We are therefore told that it is quite evident that there is a mistake in the Carthaginian Calendar under the entry for December 27.

We ought to read : " St. John and St. James, the Apostles whom Herod slew " (*quos Herodes occidit*).

The first part of this emendation we may perhaps admit to be correct, because John the Baptist has his own day in this very calendar on June 24, and we still keep St. John the Evangelist's day on December 27, and this custom is of very early origin. But the second part of the emendation is entirely without support and is made solely in the interest of the theory which we are discussing. Indeed, this martyr-ology when amended in the conjectural and wholly inadmissible manner is the *only piece of direct evidence* available for the statement so confidently made by some critics that John was put to death early in Jeru-salem, perhaps by Herod.

And this is historical criticism—to doubt and re-ject nearly contemporary evidence and to accept evi-dence in a document compiled four hundred years after the event, and then needing to be amended to make it fit in with the exigencies of the theory !

We leave our readers to judge of the value of a theory that needs evidence and support of this kind.

Those who are interested in the matter will find it fully treated in Dr. J. Armitage Robinson's book on *The Historical Character of St. John's Gospel*, and in the third volume of Dr. Stanton's *Gospels as Historical Documents*.

Their arguments may be summarised as follows : It was the custom in the Eastern Church to treat Stephen, John, James, Paul and Peter with special honour, and for this reason their festivals were kept immediately after Christmas.

This is shown by quotations from a Syriac homily by Aphrahat (A.D. 344), and also from the sermons of Gregory of Nyssa (Robinson, *op. cit.* pp. 71, 74–78 ; Migne, *Patrologia Græca*, vol. 46, cols. 730, 789).

One passage from Gregory's sermon for the day after St. Stephen's Day is especially noteworthy in this connection.

He says : " To this Stephen all the precious stones were immediately joined together, the most divine heralds of the Gospels ; after them the martyrs, and after them again those that have shone with saving virtue—principally those commemorated at the present season who flash forth the beauty of piety far and brightly, I mean Peter and James and John, the leaders of the Apostolic harmony and the crowns of the Church's glory."

These, he adds, have obtained in various ways the honour of martyrdom : Peter crucified head downwards ; James beheaded ; " John suffering divers trials [here follows an obscure passage which seems to refer to the tradition that the Apostle was dipped in boiling oil at Rome] is numbered with the martyrs, for with those that reckon aright martyrdom is judged not from the result of the suffering, but from the desire of the choice."

It is quite plain from this passage that Gregory, who preached these sermons towards the end of the fourth century, did not think that the inclusion of the name of John in this series of festivals proved that he suffered a violent death. Indeed, he says the exact contrary, namely, that the sufferings of John did not result in his death.

As for the reference in the Syrian calendar to James and John " at Jerusalem," which seems to be parallel to the reference to Peter and Paul " at Rome," where it was then universally believed that these Apostles had met their deaths, there must be some omission or confusion. The Syriac calendar is an abridgement of a Greek calendar, and has been carelessly made.

The Greek original had affinities to the Hieronymian calendar which was used in the West. In this calendar we read on December 27, " Adsumptio (or in some MSS. depositio or dormitio) S. Johannis Evangelistæ apud Ephesum et ordinatio episcopatus S. Jacobi fratris Domini" (Stanton, *op. cit.* p. 114).

According to this calendar the day was kept as the memorial of the death of John at Ephesus by natural causes—the legend of his bodily assumption is a late fabrication which crept into the manuscripts.

There also seems to have been a widespread confusion between the festival of James the son of Zebedee and that of James the brother of the Lord.

In the East, James, the Lord's brother, had his festival in some calendars on December 27, in others on December 26 or 28. The festival of James the son of Zebedee was generally held in April, because he was put to death at the Passover (Acts xiii. 3).

Dr. Kellner, of Bonn, in his book on the *Ecclesiastical Year* (p. 257), in a passage which has nothing whatever to do with the present controversy, says that the reference in the Syrian calendar may be to the consecration of a church in Jerusalem by the Empress Helena, which was dedicated to James and John.

This is quite probable. The confusion in which the whole matter is involved serves to show how uncertain a basis on which to rest any historical theory is to be found in the martyrologies, especially when the theory in question contradicts practically all the other evidence available.

And yet Schwartz has the effrontery to say, " The martyrdom of John and James rests on the sure and impregnable witness of Papias and the Syrian Martyrology " (quoted by Nolloth, *op. cit.* p. 73).

If he stated the full truth he would have had to say that it rested on the evidence of a late and self-contradictory compilation of uncertain authorship in which a quotation was made from an author of " small intelligence " which contains a statement which contradicts all the other available evidence, and also on a modern textual emendation of a fourth-century martyrology.

To sum up : the decision of the question depends on whether we prefer the nearly contemporary direct evidence of Irenæus, the greater part of whose works we possess, or the evidence of Papias, of whose works we possess very little, as quoted by two late and unsatisfactory compilers. Most of the other evidence which has been brought forward on either side is only important as confirming in a greater or less degree the evidence of the primary witnesses.

We must add, however, that the universal tradition of the Church is on the side of Irenæus, and that the Johannine literature always remains to be accounted for.

We should not have heard much of Philip and Georgius if it had not been for the bearing of their statement on the authorship of this literature. It is significant that their evidence is only regarded as important by writers who on various grounds, scientific, philosophical or linguistic, believe that the Gospel cannot have been written by the son of Zebedee.

As Bishop Headlam says : " The evidence on which this new theory is supported would be treated with contempt if it were brought forward in support of a traditional opinion" (*Miracles of the New Testament*, p. 179).

But the point of view from which this question is now generally regarded may be judged from the following quotation from the last volume of Dr. Stanton's *Gospels as Historical Documents* : " Trustworthy as the tradition of Apostolic authorship may be held to be, this authorship could not thereby be proved, if the character of the Gospel should appear to be incompatible with it."

With this we would contrast the words of Dom Chapman in his *John the Presbyter* : " A person who imagines that the authorship of a work can be denied entirely apart from all external evidence on the ground of his own *a priori* notion of what the author, otherwise unknown, ought to have written, may be a scientifically impartial theologian, for all I know, but he is not a critic at all."

The real difficulty is here. The question cannot, apparently, be approached simply as an historical problem and discussed with an open mind.

By many it is considered impossible that any man could have represented another man, whom he had known intimately, as speaking of himself or of his relationship to God in the way in which the writer of the Fourth Gospel represents Christ speaking.

We are told that Westcott has not grappled with the question as to whether it was probable that one of the Twelve would have so presented his testimony, and, apparently on this account, all the arguments that he brought forward in favour of the Apostolic authorship of this Gospel are now generally ignored, or certainly left unanswered.

We doubt if this question presented any serious difficulty at all to a man who had the sort of faith in Christ that Westcott had.

We may freely allow that it is incredible that any man should have spoken of and described another man, who had been his personal friend, in the way in which the writer of the Fourth Gospel describes and speaks of Jesus.

But—

"What if this friend happened to be—God ? "

This is still the question behind all discussions of the authorship of the Fourth Gospel, and it seems as if it were not without influence in the discussion of such a simple historical problem as whether the son of Zebedee was ever in Asia or not.

APPENDIX I

THE Dean of Wells has kindly drawn my attention to an article by Mr. Lockton in the August number of *Theology*, 1922.

This deals with the extract from Philip of Side quoted on p. 12. He gives the words which stand as the preface to this fragment as follows : " A collection of different narratives from the birth of our Lord according to the flesh and onwards beginning with the first book of the Ecclesiastical History of Eusebius Pamphili." This preface is given in the original Greek, with comments on the whole passage, by Dom Chapman, *John the Presbyter*, pp. 95 *sqq.* and nowhere else, not even by Lightfoot.

Both Mr. Lockton and Dom Chapman think that the epitomiser of Philip did not have the books of Papias at all, but was only depending on second-hand information, for (1) he states that Eusebius is his authority, and it is plain that almost everything in this passage can be found in Eusebius ; (2) he puts in the mouth of Papias a statement quoted by Eusebius (*H.E.* iv. 3) from Quadratus and makes nonsense of it by making Quadratus say that those Christ raised from the dead lived until the time of Hadrian (A.D. 117), while what Quadratus did say was that some of them lived until his own time.

It is obvious that the first seven lines of the fragment as printed in this book are taken from Eusebius iii. 36 and 39. The passage introduced by the words " He says " is obviously suggested by Eusebius iii. 25 and vii. 25. If it contained the words of Papias it would be a proof that he considered that the Gospel and First Epistle were by the Apostle.

54

There are no words to represent "he says" in the Greek. It is necessary to insert them in English because in the Greek the following words are in *oratio obliqua*, and are thereby shown to be a quotation from an author unnamed.

In the original there follow some words which are omitted on p. 12 : "And Papias was mistaken about the Millennium, and Irenæus in consequence also erred." These are taken from Eusebius iii. 39. Then follow the crucial words : "Papias in his second book says that John the Divine and James his brother were killed by the Jews." Mr. Lockton suggests with good reason that this careless epitomiser is again misquoting Eusebius here, because the account of the death of James the Brother of the Lord at the hands of the Jews occurs in the Second Book of his History.

It might also be suggested that, as the name of Papias occurs just above in the MS., the copyist may have repeated it here or introduced it intentionally to supply the (possibly) omitted subject of the verb translated "says."

The rest of the fragment contains statements which are taken from Eusebius with a few unimportant additions.

If Mr. Lockton's suggestion is correct, the whole basis for the theory of the martyrdom of John is destroyed, for the interpolator of Georgius almost certainly copied this passage from "Philip." As Mr. Lockton says, this controversy might have been avoided if the learned scholars who started it had only taken the trouble to look at the context of the passage on which they seized so joyfully. One could hardly have a better example of the onesidedness of the critical school in Germany or of the sheeplike and trustful docility with which certain British scholars follow them.

E

APPENDIX II

ON THE INTERPOLATION IN THE CHRONICLE OF GEORGIUS HAMARTOLUS

A TRANSLATION of the text of Georgius as given by de Boor and a translation of the text as it stands in the *Codex Coislinianus* are given below in parallel columns.

He (John) was the sole survivor of the Twelve Apostles, and after writing his Gospel fell asleep in peace. About whom the well-informed Eusebius says in his *Ecclesiastical History :* " Thomas received by lot Parthia, but John Asia, where also he made his residence, and died at Ephesus." And again : " In addition to these things, then, John also, the Evangelist, dies at Ephesus in Asia, and is buried there by the faithful of that place."

He (John) was the sole survivor of the Twelve Apostles, and after writing his Gospel RECEIVED THE HONOUR OF MARTYRDOM. FOR PAPIAS, BISHOP OF HIERAPOLIS, WHO WAS AN EYEWITNESS OF HIM, IN THE SECOND BOOK OF THE ORACLES OF THE LORD, SAYS THAT HE WAS KILLED BY THE JEWS, etc. AND INDEED (καὶ μὲν δὴ καὶ) the well-informed Eusebius also in his *Ecclesiastical History*, says : " Thomas received by lot Parthia, but John Asia, where also he made his residence, and died at Ephesus."

De Boor's text of Georgius, which is in the left-hand column above, makes good sense, and the quotations from

Eusebius illustrate the statement made that the Apostle died in peace. In the interpolated text the words "about whom" (περὶ οὗ καὶ) have been altered into "and indeed" (καὶ μὲν δὴ καὶ). The quotation from Eusebius in this text completely fails to support the statement that John received the honour of martyrdom, in support of which it is alleged. There could hardly be a plainer case of interpolation. Professor Zahn, the Dean of Wells, and Dr. Brooke all regard this passage as an interpolation. The first two are confident that it is so, the last mentioned thinks that it is probably so.

On the other hand, it will be found that neither Dr. Moffatt, Dr. Charles, Dr. Burney, Dr. Latimer Jackson, nor Canon Streeter makes it clear in any way that there is any question that this passage, on which so much depends, is an interpolation. Dr. Charles and Dr. Latimer Jackson say that it is the reading of one manuscript of Georgius ; Dr. Moffatt says that it is the reading of the best manuscript ; Dr. Burney and Canon Streeter simply attribute the passage to Georgius. A passage in support of a theory which requires to be introduced with such reticence is evidently of rather a doubtful character.

Those who wish to form an intelligent opinion of the way in which such matters as these are handled by critics are strongly advised to read the pages in the *Introduction to the N.T.* by Dr. Moffatt, and the *Commentary on the Apocalypse* by Dr. Charles, which deal with this particular part of the question in the light of the facts stated above.

APPENDIX III

M. LEPIN treats the matter generally as follows: If the words of Christ were a *vaticinium post eventum*, it is necessary to suppose that the bloody martyrdom of the sons of Zebedee made a great impression in the Church, so great that it was treated as an event worthy to have been foretold by Christ. How is it, then, that the martyrdom of James is the only one mentioned in the tradition, and that it seems to have been assumed by the author of the last chapter of the Fourth Gospel that the belief prevailing in the Church was that John would survive until the Parousia ?

The words of the Gospel about the cup and the baptism, if they had been intended in this sense, would have kept the tradition alive.

There are many instances of saints in the early Church being credited with violent martyrdom in the traditions, but none of their being deprived of this credit. Reville agrees with Lepin in this (*Quatr. Ev.*, p. 21). Lepin also quotes the two following passages :

"The Lord made allusion to their death, for James had his head cut off, and John endured death in many ways " (*Chrys. in Mt. Hom.* viii.).

According to Funk, *Patres Apost.* ii. 288, Victor of Capua attributed to Polycarp this explanation of the prophecy of the "cup" : James will end his life by bloody martyrdom, his brother John after having suffered persecutions and exiles will not be martyred himself, but Christ nevertheless esteems as a martyr that man who in his soul is disposed to martyrdom.

Victor is, of course, a late author, but his reference to Polycarp is at least as valuable as the very doubtful references of Philip and Georgius to Papias.

It is also interesting to note that in *De Anima*, L., in a context where he has been speaking of the translation of Enoch and Elijah, Tertullian says : " Even John underwent death, although concerning him there had prevailed an underground expectation that he would remain alive until the coming of the Lord."

" The Evangelist did not speculate on the origin of his theological thought any more than St. Paul. ' He was ready,' you say, ' to see Christ and to understand the Gospel in the manner in which he sets it forth. He persuaded himself, without any further reasoning, that this manner was the best and true one and that it contains fundamentally that which Christ wished to teach the Apostles. In this conviction he wrote in order that men might believe, as he did, that Jesus was the Christ, the Son of God. . . . Since he has told us in express terms what was the object of his work, it is waste time to look for others which had no influence on him.'

" Stay a moment. You throw us here into absolute hallucination and you assure us that the author of the Fourth Gospel had no other object. . . . The author tells us that he wrote that Jesus is the Christ, the Son of God, but he does not tell us that he imagined the miracles of the man born blind, of the multiplication of the loaves, and of the resurrection of Lazarus ; he does not tell us that he invented the conversations with the Samaritan woman and Nicodemus with the Saviour out of his own head ; he does not tell us that he imagined the discourses that Jesus pronounced, or the great scenes that preceded, accompanied, or followed His death on Calvary. It is you who say these strange things and not he. . . .

" According to you the most beautiful book in the world is accounted for by the sublime hallucination of a man who has never seen or heard Christ and for whom historical truth did not exist. He imagined a Christ, the Word of God, and having imagined Him wished to make Him an object of worship.

" Then he wrote the most poignant and ideal romance that has ever been written.

" After writing it, this anonymous person assumed the name of the Apostle John and signed his book with it. He published it ; and all his contemporaries believed that it was the work of the Apostle John and accepted it as such. This forgery, which no one suspected, the Church has naïvely accepted for nineteen hundred years. But now you have arisen to put an end to this error."

THE ABBÉ FRÉMONT, *Lettres à l'Abbé Loisy*, pp. 145, 146.

"Now when they saw the boldness of Peter and John, and perceived that they were unlearned and ignorant men, they marvelled ; and took knowledge of them, that they had been with Jesus."—ACTS IV. 13.

"History is the endeavour to find out what actually happened, not to force on the evidence an *a priori* point of view, however brilliantly chosen."—B. H. Streeter, *The Four Gospels*, p. 543.

"Criticism has to resolve this enigma, how an evangelical tradition so certainly independent was able to take its place alongside the Synoptists, unless it rested on the authority of an eyewitness."—Bousset, *Offerbarung*, p. 45.

"Si le miracle et l'inspiration de certains livres sont choses réelles notre methode est détestable."—Renan, *Vie de Jesus*, ix.

"A cette hauteur de contemplation mystique, il ne discerne pas ce que le Christ historique a dit et fait, de ce que lui-même fait dire et faire son Christ : il voit comme réels les discours qu'il lui prête et les signes où il incarne la doctrine des discours : il les voit et il les y assiste dans ce disciple idéal qui ne se distingue plus de lui-même."—Loisy, *Les Quatre Evangiles*, p. 86.

"Si Jésus n'est pas le Fils de Dieu, Dieu et homme, il est bien près d'être un illuminé   Les eschatologistes purs n'aiment pas à prononcer ce mot, mais ils concèdent que Jésus n'a pas d'autre utilité pour nous que par l'impulsion qu'il a donnée aux idées religieuses de son temps."—Lagrange, *L'Evangile selon St. Marc*, p. lxi.

"A world-wide religion which for more than thirty centuries has been taking hold on the most highly developed races could not have had its origin in mere mental disease."—Sanday, *Inspiration*, p. 394.

JOHN THE SON OF ZEBEDEE AND THE FOURTH GOSPEL

WE hope that the foregoing dissertation has convinced our readers that the early death of John is not a matter of such certainty as to make it impossible to think of him as the author of the Fourth Gospel.

We are now obliged, for the sake of argument, to ask that it may be further conceded that it is possible that he may have lived at Ephesus and written his Gospel there.

We are told by Dean Inge that "hardly any competent scholars" are now willing to support the traditional view of the authorship, and in many recent books, such as Canon Streeter's *Four Gospels*, the whole tenor of the argument is influenced by the assumption that it is not only improbable, but impossible that the Apostle should have written the Gospel.

At the very end of his book this author states that any critic who knows his business before giving a verdict in favour of the apostolic authorship of a Gospel will require an attestation stronger than a classical scholar would think necessary for a work attributed to Xenophon or Plato : he also adds—"the burden of proof is on those who assert the traditional authorship of Matthew and John" (p. 562).

Dr. Stanton in his *Gospels as Historical Documents*

expresses a similar idea in rather a different tone :
" It must be regretfully allowed that those who believe
themselves entitled to speak in the name of criticism
for the most part deny that the Fourth Gospel has any
independent value in the historical sense. That is, it
adds nothing trustworthy to the statements of the
Synoptists."

Now if this view represents the truth, we must, of
course, accept it ; but first we may be allowed to ask
who are the persons who call upon us to accept it, and
what are their credentials ?

Dr. Stanton classifies them in rather a curious way.
He calls them " those who believe themselves entitled
to speak in the name of criticism." That is to say,
persons who claim for themselves the right to speak
on these matters, not necessarily those who have the
best right to speak.

We have been examining the proofs brought
forward by some of these writers with regard to the
alleged early death of the Apostle, and we have found
that not only do they lack cogency, but also that in
many cases they are based on serious over- or under-
statements of the facts. With regard, therefore, to
these further allegations, namely, that the burden of
proof is on those who maintain that the Gospel has
an apostolic author and that it has no historic value,
we ask leave respectfully to withhold our assent until
we have examined the matter somewhat further.

In the words of Dr. Johnson, when confronted with
a writer who made unsupported assertions, we shall
pay attention not to what the critics shall say, but to
what they shall prove.

The attempt to foreclose inquiry either by confronting supporters of the traditional view with the
number and " competency " of their opponents, or by
ignoring all arguments except those brought forward

by the critical school, as unworthy of discussion or even mention, is much to be deprecated.

The fate of the theories of the Tübingen School, whose members might certainly have been described in their day as " those who believed themselves entitled to speak in the name of criticism," may well make us hesitate before we accept a similar body of critics in our own day as infallible and irrefutable.

As far, at least, as the sojourn of the Apostle at Ephesus is concerned, it was Renan and not Bishop Westcott who wrote that " it remains probable " and that " les chances de vérité sont encore en faveur de la tradition " in spite of " the scorn of a young presumptuous school in the eyes of which every theory is proved, provided that it is negative, and which peremptorily treats as ignorant those that do not immediately accept its exaggerations " (*L'Antichrist*, p. 558).

In considering the question of the authorship of an ancient book proofs of two kinds may be used— external proofs and internal proofs. External proofs are sought in the testimony which other writers give to their knowledge of the fact that the book in question was written by the author whose name it bears. Failing this, testimony to the mere fact that the book existed at a certain date may have its value.

Internal proofs are drawn from the congruity of the contents of the book itself with the character, the circumstances and the training of the supposed author, and from its agreement with the known characteristics of the time and place when and in which it is supposed to have been written. It may further have to be considered if the book has been in any way edited or interpolated and, if so, by whom, when and why.

If it can be shown, as Bentley showed in the case of the Epistles of Phalaris, that the book which is under consideration was never mentioned till centuries after the supposed author's death; if it can be shown that it contains obvious anachronisms, or references to things that could never have been thought of at the time when the supposed author lived, then the book is rightly condemned as spurious on sound critical principles.

If, however, the critic goes on, as Bentley did in dealing with the *Paradise Lost* of Milton, to re-write or omit passages in a book about the authorship and transmission of which there is good external evidence, because in his opinion these passages are not worthy of the poet's genius and, therefore, cannot have been written by him, then his criticisms must be received with extreme caution. They may be amply justified and worthy of acceptance, but they are, and always must remain, purely subjective—that is, they represent the critic's opinion of what the author might be expected to have written, and nothing more.

External evidence, where it may be had, is more convincing than internal, because it is objective and the inferences that may be drawn from it are less likely to be distorted by the prejudices and opinions of the critic. Where, however, external evidence is scanty, as it is in the question which we are at present discussing, it may be and is interpreted in quite different ways by critics who set out with opposite presuppositions.   How far this is the case may be judged from the following quotation from von Soden's *Urchristliche Literaturgeschichte*: "There is absolutely no reliable attestation in favour of the hypothesis that prevailed from the end of the third century that John, one of the Twelve Apostles, ever lived or worked at Ephesus. This hypothesis rests on the confusion that arose between John the Elder and the Apostle of the same name. The evidence in favour of the Elder is as reliable as it can possibly be. The confusion arose in the third century and is characteristic of an epoch that abounds in gross historical errors." Again, " It is only in the third century that John of Ephesus is called an Apostle. The second century knew absolutely nothing of John the Apostle " (pp. 214, 215). This needs no comment to those who have read the first part of this book with any attention.

It seems inevitable that the question of the apostolic authorship of the Fourth Gospel should be finally decided by internal evidence.

No one maintains that the external evidence is in itself decisive against the Apostle's being the author of the Gospel, except those who hold it to be proved that he was put to death in Palestine at an early date and those who treat the external evidence after the manner of von Soden.

Probably most other critics would admit that the external evidence is sufficient to make the apostolic authorship of the Gospel probable, IF ONLY ITS CONTENTS WERE DIFFERENT FROM WHAT THEY ACTUALLY ARE.

Many of those who do not accept the apostolic authorship approach the subject with a strong presupposition that it is most unlikely that one of the Twelve could have produced a representation of Christ such as is found in this Gospel. Its contents are treated as " Johannine theology " and as being a thoroughly idealised representation of what our Lord actually did and said. Others think that even if some better educated and more distantly removed follower might have produced the Gospel, yet it could not have been produced by the son of Zebedee, who was a Galilean fisherman, not at all versed in Rabbinic lore or Greek philosophy, and who was, moreover, a bigoted Jew who up to middle life was a " pillar " of the Church of Jerusalem.

In reading books in which the apostolic authorship is denied or minimised it is always necessary to consider how far the conclusion is founded on external or really cogent internal evidence and how far it is the result of the critic's having first made up his mind that the Gospel cannot possibly have been written by the son of Zebedee, or any other personal follower of Christ.

Before going further we should like to make clear what we understand by " cogent internal evidence." If it could be shown that the Gospel contains some glaring anachronisms, or that it was written by one who knew nothing about Jerusalem or the Jews of the first century, we should consider this cogent internal evidence against the apostolic authorship. Many attempts have been made to demonstrate that the Gospel does contain anachronisms and that it displays ignorance of Jewish customs and places, but these have so far failed that such resolute opponents of the apostolic authorship as Dr. Charles, Dr. Burney, Canon Streeter and Dean Inge all admit that the author was a Jew, and Dr. Burney has written a book to show that he was a Palestinian Jew.

Those, however, who desire to know how strong the internal evidence is that the Gospel was written by a Jew who lived in Palestine in the time of our Lord, should refer to Bishop Lightfoot's comparatively little-known essays reprinted in his *Biblical Essays*. It is astonishing, but none the less true, that many recent writers have taken upon themselves to write about the authenticity of the Fourth Gospel without the least reference to the weighty arguments contained in the second of these essays.

It is therefore clear that, as far as many recent writers are concerned, the refusal to recognise the Apostle as the author of the Gospel does not rest on the sure ground of obvious anachronism and incongruity with the surroundings in which the book is supposed to have been written, but on something far more uncertain and precarious, namely, on the general opinion of these writers that it is unlikely to the verge of impossibility that one of the Twelve should have presented his testimony to Christ in the form in which it is presented in the Fourth Gospel.

We believe that all the most important documents on which the external evidence for the authenticity of the Gospel is founded have been printed in the first dissertation in this book. Since that was written an important book has been published by Canon Streeter on the Four Gospels, several chapters of which are devoted to a discussion of the authorship and value of the Fourth Gospel. This book is written in a striking and thoroughly modern style and may attract many whom the usual type of book on New Testament criticism would repel. It is said to be written for " educated laymen " and for " theological students." As such readers are not necessarily well acquainted with all the intricacies of early Church history, it seems desirable to warn them that this book presents only one side of the case with regard to the Johannine question. The arguments presented are, moreover, by no means so original or novel as might be supposed from the manner of their presentation ; they have nearly all been used before by such writers as Strauss, Renan, Loisy, Schmiedel, Harnack and Schwartz. Those who wish to see these questions treated at length will find practically all Canon Streeter's arguments set out and effectively answered in *L'Origine du Quatrième Evangile*, by M. Lepin, which was published by Letouzey et Ané, of Paris, in 1907.

As, however, every one has not the time to read so large a book, we purpose in the following dissertation to deal with the arguments which Canon Streeter offers to us.

Canon Streeter begins with the last two verses of the Gospel (p. 430). He is delighted and apparently surprised to find that " so conservative a critic as Westcott " is willing to admit that these verses were not written by the author of the Gospel, and therefore come under the category of external evidence.

One would have thought that this was an admission that any one of ordinary common sense would willingly make without the concurrence of " the most cautious and conservative of scholars."

Why, then, asks our author, were these verses added ? Obviously because certain persons dissented from the view as to the authorship which they express. As it is unlikely that there would be any such dissent at the time and in the place where the Gospel was first published, they were probably added AT A LATER DATE AND IN ANOTHER LOCALITY. It need hardly be said that in making these assumptions our author is *not* following in the steps of " the most cautious and conservative of critics," to whose commentary interested readers would do well to refer.

Canon Streeter seems to have forgotten that in the first chapter of his book he has proved to his own satisfaction that there was a feeling of uneasiness about the statements contained in the Fourth Gospel when they came to be compared with those of Mark and Matthew in the very place and at the very time in which and when the Gospel was composed. If his argument in this chapter is sound, it must follow also that the author of the Fourth Gospel cannot have been regarded in Ephesus as a thoroughly reliable person, since he had to defend himself from charges of inaccuracy.

He also seems to forget that in chap. xvi. he has built up an elaborate fantasy in which he describes

the author of the Fourth Gospel as the First of the
Modernists, who was looked upon with grave suspicion
by the old-fashioned church-goers of the day. It is
true that he admits (p. 467) that in this last-mentioned
chapter he is straying from the paths of " stern
historical method " and giving the rein to his imagination, still he obviously wishes us to believe that his
fantasy represents a possible state of affairs.

We must assume, however, that in the first chapter
he is following the paths of the " stern historical
method," for he there quotes the well-known passages
in which Eusebius reports the traditions that he derived
from Papias about the Gospels of Mark and Matthew
(p. 19). In accordance with an idea put forward by
Schwartz, he believes that he has discovered the true
meaning of these passages and explained " the extraordinary fact that the earliest allusion in Christian
literature to the Gospels is an endeavour to minimise
their accuracy and apostolic authority " (p. 21).

The first passage quoted from Papias may be summarised as follows : John the Elder said that Mark
was a follower of Peter and wrote down accurately
all that he remembered of Peter's teaching, but not
in the correct order, for he neither heard the Lord
nor followed Him. Mark, however, made no mistake
when he wrote down his recollections in this way, for
he was careful to omit nothing and not to set down
any false statements.

In the second passage Papias states (he does not
say on whose authority) that Matthew composed the
oracles in the Hebrew language and that each man
interpreted them as he could (Eusebius, *H.E.* iii. 39).

Canon Streeter believes that the person to whom
Papias refers as the " Elder " wrote the Fourth Gospel.
He also assumes that BOTH the pieces of tradition
quoted above came to Papias from the " Elder,"

although Papias only attributes to him the tradition relative to Mark. He thinks that when the Fourth Gospel was first published at Ephesus it was received with suspicion on two grounds, first it contradicted the order of the events of the life of Christ to which the Ephesian Christians were accustomed from hearing the Gospel of Mark read in church, secondly it substituted nebulous teaching with regard to the coming of the Paraclete for the doctrine of the immediate and visible return of Christ which was so plainly taught in the " prophetic * utterances " of Matthew.

In order to defend the accuracy of his representation of the life and teaching of Christ, the " Elder " set himself to disparage the old-fashioned Gospel of Mark. He stated that Mark was correct as to the facts, but weak as to the order of events, for he had never been a personal follower of the Lord, while he, the author of the Fourth Gospel, claimed to have been one of the early disciples.

The " Elder " dealt with Matthew (according to Canon Streeter) by pointing out that his collection of " prophetic utterances " was originally written in Hebrew and that there was no authorised translation of it. Consequently, if there was anything in the Greek Gospel which was current under the name of Matthew which conflicted with his own account of the teaching of Christ about the future, or perplexed the weaker brethren, this must be put down to the fact that the Gospel was only a translation from the Hebrew and, perhaps, not a good one. Thus, according to the theory brought forward by Canon Streeter in the first chapter of his book, the author of the Fourth Gospel disposed of the criticisms which were made against his representation of the life of Christ as soon as it was published.

* Canon Streeter translates the much-disputed word $\lambda \acute{o} \gamma \iota a$ in this way.

We do not quote this extraordinary piece of ex-position because we agree with it, but because it effectively answers Canon Streeter's statement on p. 431 that it was unlikely that any one would dissent from the view of the authorship presented in the last two verses of the Gospel in the place where the Gospel was written while the author was still alive. Those, however, who do accept the argument which we have just mentioned, and also Canon Streeter's statement on p. 479—" We may surmise that, in spite of the storm which the publication of the Gospel aroused in conservative circles, its doctrines made rapid progress elsewhere "—must admit that he has shown that serious objections were raised to the Gospel as soon as it was published and that the good faith of the author was called in question, since he had to defend himself by disparaging his predecessors. Surely the ingenious " Elder," who knew how to deal with the claims of Mark and Matthew so convincingly, could have arranged to have the useful testimonial contained in the last two verses attached to his Gospel as soon as he saw that it would be required.

Our author next goes on to observe (p. 431) that apart from the last two verses there is not a word in the Gospel to suggest that it is, or claims to be written by the Apostle John. He forgets to mention the thirty-fifth and following verses of the nineteenth chapter, which " the most cautious and conservative of critics," and many other commentators beginning with Tertullian,* believe are intended to mean that the author of the Gospel was the Beloved Disciple,

* The words of Tertullian are so important that we venture to quote them in full again :

" Was anything again concealed from John, the Lord's most beloved disciple, who used to lean on His breast, to whom alone the Lord pointed out Judas as the traitor and whom He commended to Mary as a son in His own stead ? Of what could He have meant those to be ignorant, to whom He even exhibited His own glory with

who stood beside the Cross. It is true that this
interpretation is disputed by many less cautious
critics ; but in a book intended for readers who are
not specialists such things should not be passed over.

Then the well-worn and often-answered objection
is brought forward that, as it is unlikely that John
would speak of himself as " the disciple whom Jesus
loved," the Gospel cannot possibly have been written
by him. This quite imaginary difficulty seems so
decisive to Canon Streeter that he assumes everywhere
else that the Gospel cannot have been written by the
Apostle.

Then the whole question is quietly begged in the
words : " If the Fourth Gospel had come down to us
AS ORIGINALLY PUBLISHED without the last two verses,
every one everywhere would have taken it for granted
that the author intended to distinguish himself from
the Beloved Disciple, and we should have inferred
that its author stood in the same relationship to the
Beloved Disciple as Mark, the author of another of
the Gospels, stood to Peter * " (p. 432). It being now
assumed that the Gospel, when it left the hands of
its author, was anonymous, and that the attribution to
the Beloved Disciple was added " at a later date and

Moses and Elias, and the Father's voice moreover from heaven ? "
(*De Præscriptione*, xxii.).

In a passage referring to the translation of Enoch and Elijah
he says, " Even John underwent death, although there had prevailed
concerning him an underground expectation that he would remain
until the coming of the Lord " (*De Anima*, L.).

It should be noted that this clear testimony that Tertullian
believed that the Apostle John was the Beloved Disciple and the
author of the Gospel, and that the last chapter of the Gospel was an
integral part of it, must represent not only his own opinion, but also
the general opinion of the time both among the orthodox members
of the Church and heretics, and that it cannot have been an opinion
of recent growth, since he appeals to it without any apparent fear
of contradiction.

With this compare the words of von Soden on p. 65.

* So Renan.

in another locality," it is quite easy to go on to assume that this attribution is a mistake. This is accordingly done, and we are assured that the Gospel was not written by the Beloved Disciple, but by one to whom this disciple was " an object of reverent admiration " (p. 432).

Who, then, was the Beloved Disciple : John the son of Zebedee, or a purely ideal figure—the perfect disciple who alone understood the mind of Christ ? Canon Streeter answers that BOTH these figures were included in the conception. John must have been the real figure behind the ideal. Peter, James and John in the Marcan story form the inner circle of the Twelve. Since the Beloved Disciple is one whom the Church expected to tarry until the Lord's coming, James is ruled out by his early death, while Peter's infirmities are too conspicuous a feature in the tradition to make it possible for him to be selected as the ideal : only John is left (p. 433).

From the standpoint of much modern " criticism," this is a remarkable admission. It would seem as if Canon Streeter did not agree with those who would regard the whole of the last chapter of the Gospel as an imaginary picture composed much later than the rest. In the end, however (p. 472), he almost comes round to this view, rather to the detriment of his present argument.

As for the story of the early death of John by violence, which he is very anxious to believe and which he ends in virtually accepting (pp. 435, 452), he fits this in as best he can by suggesting that the Apostle may have been killed in A.D. 66.

How, in this case, the Church came to believe that John, and apparently only John, would tarry until the Second Coming he does not stay to explain.

Next he describes what he supposes the relationship

between the author of the Gospel and the Beloved Disciple to have been (p. 433).

The author MAY have met the disciple in his youth and conceived a "mystical veneration" for him. Elsewhere (pp. 418, 456) he suggests that the author was only twelve years old at the Crucifixion, which he may have seen, and could therefore be described as "one who had seen the Lord" without undue exaggeration or sacrifice of strict veracity. "We need not suppose that he had seen a great deal of John, or that more than a small number of the facts recorded in the Gospel were derived from him ; most of them, indeed, we have seen reason to believe came to him by way of Mark and Luke. We need only postulate for him a connection with the Apostle and an attitude to his memory comparable to that of Irenæus towards Polycarp. A brief and, as it seemed in the halo of later recollection, a wonderful connection with the Apostle—perhaps also a few never-to-be-forgotten words of Christ derived from his lips—would make the attitude towards the Beloved Disciple expressed in the Gospel psychologically explicable" (p. 433).

On the strength of this mystic veneration for one whom Canon Streeter, with unconscious deference to a discredited tradition, still calls "the aged Apostle," and some facts derived from Mark and Luke, this wonderful boy produced the Fourth Gospel in his old age. If Canon Streeter had been a Father of the second century, and if this account of the origin of the Fourth Gospel had been preserved for us as the only surviving fragment of his writings, would not any reasonable critic have been justified in inferring from it that he "knew nothing" of our Fourth Gospel ?

Is it possible to imagine a person less likely to have produced the Gospel as we know it than one who had only seen Christ on the Cross as a boy, who had seen very little of the Beloved Disciple and derived from him very few of the facts that he records, but was mainly dependent for them on the Gospels of Mark and Luke.

In other places in his book Canon Streeter amplifies the account that he here gives of the sources of the Fourth Gospel in a remarkable manner. He has built his argument in chap. i. on the fact that the author of the Fourth Gospel knew the Gospel according to Matthew and disparaged it (p. 21). On pp. 403, 419 he allows that the author had " a good pilgrim's knowledge " of Palestine and, although probably not a Palestinian Jew, was " versed in Rabbinic tradition and the usages of the Temple system."

We are still left in the dark as to the source from which the author derived the many incidents and discourses which he could not possibly have taken from the Synoptists, except for a vague reference to " Jerusalem tradition " (p. 418), and the statement on p. 417 that " it is in the direction of the personality of the author that we are to look for an explanation of the major divergences of the Fourth Gospel from the Synoptists." Taken in connection with much else that we read in this book, we can only suppose that this is an involved way of saying that most of the incidents and discourses that are not derived from the Synoptists have their origin in the imagination of the author. Again, on p. 417 we are amazed to read that if we " deduct from John what seems to be derived from Mark and Luke, only a few odd incidents remain." This is the first time that we have ever seen that portion of the story of the life of Christ which is peculiar to the Fourth Gospel dismissed as " a few odd incidents."

What a peculiar personality the author of the Fourth Gospel is supposed to have had by those who look upon him as a mystic and a seer, but not in any sense as a historian, may best be judged from the following quotations from Loisy.

" One would say that allegorical invention sprang up spontaneously in him by means of a powerful inspiration. There is nothing to wonder at in this because the author is a great mystic, the first and greatest of Christian mystics. However, it is not enough to say this, one must add that he was also a prophet. The Fourth Gospel might well be a vision." " The author of these pictures was half, if not altogether, unconscious of the distance which separates the events recorded by himself from the events recorded by his predecessors. At least the depth of mystic sentiment, the intense force of imaginative representations and the theological spirit seem to have brought him to a sort of indifference for accuracy and even for historical reality which are nearly equivalent to a radical incapacity for feeling, inquiring after and expressing this reality " * (*Le Quatrième Evangile*, pp. 659, 660).

Modern criticism, compelled to acknowledge that the Gospel was written by one who was at least in

* It was of explanations of the origin of the Gospels of this kind that Renan wrote : " At the bottom all this symbolism is the counterpart of the mythism of Strauss—an expedient of theologians at bay, taking refuge in allegory, myth and symbol " (*Vie de Jésus*, p. 508). And again : " We must then choose between two possibilities : either to recognise John, the son of Zebedee, as the author of the Fourth Gospel, or to regard this Gospel as an apocryphal work composed by a person who wished to pass it off as the work of John the son of Zebedee. There is no question here of legends, the productions of the crowd for which no one has any responsibility. A man who, to gain belief for his writings, deceives the public not only as to his name, but also as to the value of his testimony, is not a maker of legends, he is a forger. A biographer of Francis of Assisi who lived one or two hundred years after this extraordinary man could tell the hosts of miracles, created by tradition, without, for that reason, ceasing to be perfectly straightforward and innocent. But if this biographer was to say : ' I was his intimate friend ; I was his beloved disciple ; all that I am going to tell you is true, for I saw it,' without doubt the name that would suit him would be quite different " (*Vie de Jésus*, p. 538).

contact with the apostolic generation and unwilling to shock decent human feeling by saying that the author was a deliberate forger, is forced to take refuge in this meaningless verbiage to describe the sort of man that it supposes him to have been. We are surely entitled to ask how it is that if the production of a book like the Fourth Gospel is only what is to be expected from a great Christian mystic, the supply of such books came suddenly to an end with the publication of this Gospel?

In this context it is interesting to note some further remarks by Canon Streeter which are to be found on p. 418 of his book.

He is speaking of the well-known difficulty in the way of the critical theory, namely, that the author of the Fourth Gospel would not have contradicted and corrected the account given in the Synoptists of many incidents in the life of Christ unless he had been a person who was able to speak with quite exceptional authority on account of his position and experience, such as would have been the case, if he had been the Apostle John.

"The difficulty is considerably reduced in magnitude by the result to which a critical comparison of the documents seems to point, that the only Synoptists used by John were Mark and Luke. Where John throws over the Synoptic chronology, or modifies their story in smaller details, he is not flying in the face of a universal Church tradition embodied in three separate Gospels, one of them ascribed to an Apostle : HE IS ONLY CORRECTING MARK AND LUKE, neither of which is reputed to be the work of an eyewitness. BUT IF THE AUTHOR OF THE FOURTH GOSPEL HAD HIMSELF VISITED JERUSALEM—which would naturally be regarded in the Church at large as the fountain-head of authentic tradition—he might consider himself to be in a position to correct or explain, as one having authority, the story as told in these two Gospels."

Yet on p. 416 we have been told that the Gospel of Matthew had most probably reached Ephesus, and that the "Elder" had been obliged by the theological position that he had taken up in writing his own Gospel to decline to accept it as having apostolic authority, and the argument in chap. i. results in the same conclusion.

If this is a true statement of the case, the presumptuous "Elder" was not only modifying the story of those second-hand witnesses Mark and Luke in "smaller details" on the strength of his visit to Jerusalem ("even if that meant no more than that, as a boy of twelve, taken by his father to the Passover, he had been one of the multitude who beheld the Crucifixion," p. 418), but was actually daring to refuse altogether a Gospel which came to Ephesus backed by the authority of the great Church of Antioch (as Canon Streeter supposes) and connected, at least in name, with the Apostle Matthew.

We would also ask whether Canon Streeter admits that Mark was the same person as the John Mark, mentioned in the Acts, who is there described as a resident in Jerusalem, and whether he believes that Luke ever went to Jerusalem or not? Certainly the person who wrote the "we" passages in the Acts seems to have gone to Jerusalem with Paul. However much the "Elder," as Canon Streeter would have us believe, might consider HIMSELF in a position "to correct or explain, as one having authority," the story told in the Gospels of Mark and Luke, on the strength of his visit to Jerusalem as a little boy, or on the strength of any subsequent pilgrim visit, we much doubt if any of his contemporaries would have shared his opinion of his capability or authority.

On p. 457 the author of the Gospel is described as a
man of genius to whom "the category of development
in the slow biological sense of the term" did not apply.
Surely, according to the maxims of the critical school,
it is most unscientific to postulate the existence of
genius that transcends the biological process of development, or of anything else that savours of the supernatural. To find a place for Christ in the orderly
succession of biological evolution has taxed the ingenuity of many who have set themselves to explain
away the alleged supernatural origin of Christianity.
It is really too bad of Canon Streeter to give them
another extraordinary genius to account for.

The man who evolved the Fourth Gospel out of
a casual sight of Christ on the Cross at the age
of twelve, a slight acquaintance with the "Beloved
Disciple," and a few "facts" gathered from Mark and
Luke, would certainly be a most remarkable and
unaccountable man of genius, even if it were allowed
in addition that he had a pilgrim's knowledge of
Palestine and that he was versed in Rabbinic learning
and the traditions of the Temple and was acquainted
with the Jerusalem tradition. Canon Streeter may
well say that if this was all that he had to work on,
the major divergence of the Fourth Gospel from the
Synoptists must be attributed to his personality.

Who, then, was this extraordinary genius?

Papias, in the opinion of Canon Streeter (p. 434),
informs us of the existence of a person who seems to
fulfil all the conditions required from the supposed
author of the Fourth Gospel as described above. This
person is our old friend the Elder John. Papias,
however, describes the Elder as "a disciple of
the Lord." This is rather awkward, as it hardly fits
in with the imaginary description of the author, which
we have already noted. "Since, however, Aristion and

the Elder John are distinguished by this description both from the Apostles and from the generality of less informed Christians, it must at least imply that they had seen the Lord in the flesh " (p. 434). So we get back again to the boy who is supposed to have seen our Lord on the Cross at the age of twelve.

Why the title " disciple of the Lord " should distinguish a man absolutely from the Apostles, when, as Canon Streeter admits, the " Beloved Disciple " was a name given to the Apostle John, does not appear.

If the term " disciple of the Lord " is to be emptied of all reasonable significance by such treatment as this, we can make any ancient document mean what we please by the application of similar methods of interpretation. In another place (pp. 444 *sqq.*) Canon Streeter builds an argument on the supposed fact that the title " disciple of the Lord " was so characteristic of the " Elder " and was used so often with regard to him by Polycarp, that it imprinted itself indelibly on the youthful mind of Irenæus, who for the rest of his life nearly always referred to the person who had written the Fourth Gospel as " John the disciple of the Lord," and, moreover, confused him with John the Apostle. If there is any truth in this supposition, it would seem to show that the terms " disciple of the Lord " and " Apostle " were synonymous in Asia and that people there would not have been at all likely to refer to a man who had only just seen Christ as a boy by the title of a " disciple of the Lord."

Most of those who attribute the Gospel to the " Elder " believe that he was a Jew of good education and priestly race who was at least a young man during the latter part of the life of Christ and came into personal and intelligent contact with Him in Jerusalem. But for some reason or other Canon Streeter has gone out of his way to reduce the connection between his imaginary Evangelist and Christ to the smallest possible point. Neither will he allow that he saw much of the Apostles, not even of John for whom he is supposed to have had such great reverence. Why this should be we leave to the conjectures of our readers.

Canon Streeter thinks that the Fourth Gospel reached Rome by 155, and that it was Justin Martyr (who died about 165) who first effectively commended the Gospel and the doctrine of the Logos to the Roman Church * (p. 441). The Muratorian Fragment shows that by the end of the century it was fully accepted in Rome, as it was elsewhere, as the work of the Apostle, but the emphasis with which the apostolic authorship of the Gospel is insisted on in the fragment is supposed to prove that there were some people in Rome who had not been willing to believe in its authenticity (p. 439).

He then tells the familiar story of the Alogoi and of Caius their supposed leader in Rome. With Harnack he regards these people as being good old-fashioned traditionalists who disliked the Gospel and refused to attribute it to an Apostle, because of the novel doctrines which it contained.

There is nothing new in all this. The matter has already been dealt with by Stanton in his book on the Gospels, vol. i., pp. 198 *sqq.*, and by many other writers, What is novel is the suggestion that, while Justin quotes the Synoptists freely, when he comes to the Fourth Gospel " he acts like a modern apologetic writer trying to establish the pre-existence of Christ, but, in deference to critical objections attempting to do so without reference to the Fourth Gospel "

* Loisy allows that the Gospel was known and valued in Rome from 130 (*Quatrième Evangile*, p. 14).

(p. 441). The parallel, however, hardly holds. Justin was not deferring to critical objections in avoiding the use of the Fourth Gospel, but, on Canon Streeter's own showing, he was trying to avoid wounding the susceptibilities of an old-fashioned and apparently not very influential party in the Roman Church. There is no evidence that the Alogoi were a party that contained people of special intelligence or any who had more trustworthy information about the origin of the Fourth Gospel than the rulers of the Roman Church, who seem to have accepted the Gospel without question. The very fact that they are supposed to have attributed it to Cerinthus shows their complete lack both of special information and of common sense.

A great deal is made of the fact that they were not treated as heretics and turned out of the Church, and this is supposed to prove that the authenticity of the Gospel was still quite an open question. If we think of the Alogoi as resembling the Fundamentalists of to-day, as we are encouraged to do by Canon Streeter, we shall see that their not being excommunicated is no argument at all against the authenticity of the Gospel.

The conclusion that, because Justin did not quote the Fourth Gospel as freely as the others, the Gospel was not fully accepted in his time, is also invalidated by the fact that not one of the works of Justin that we possess was intended for the edification of the faithful, still less for the instruction of the weaker brethren. The *Apologies* were written for the information of the Roman Government; the *Dialogue* for the Jews. Yet Canon Streeter says (p. 13) : " From this some scholars have inferred that while Justin himself— who had been converted to Christianity at Ephesus— accepted the Ephesian Gospel, THE ROMAN PUBLIC FOR WHOM HE WROTE did not put it quite on the same level." As far as we can see, the expression "Roman public" must mean "Roman Christians" in the context in which it stands. Is this an instance of the "creative memory" that he lays to the charge of the Fourth Evangelist and certain apologists on pp. 383 *sqq.*?

Professor Stanton has well pointed out (*Gospels*, vol. i., pp. 76 *sqq.*) that Justin in the books mentioned above used the topics of persuasion which were most likely to appeal to the persons to whom he was writing. To the Pagans he presents the moral teaching of Christ and describes His life in outline. To the Jews he quotes the Old Testament. Neither Pagans nor Jews cared or knew anything about the Apostles as individuals. He does not therefore refer to the Evangelists by name, but says that there exist books called Gospels which he describes as "Memoirs of the Apostles of Christ and of their followers." As there was not much in the distinctive teaching of the Fourth Gospel that was suited to his purpose, he made little reference to it.*

Moreover, there is some positive archæological evidence to show that the Fourth Gospel was known and valued in Rome long before the middle of the second century. In the vestibule of the Catacomb of Domitilla, which is believed by the best authorities to

* It should be noted that Tatian, the pupil of Justin, who wrote a treatise addressed to the Greeks in favour of Christianity, never mentions the authors of any of the books of the New Testament by name. The same omission is found in Tertullian's apologetic writings.

Until the discovery of the *Diatessaron* of Tatian, which is a harmony of our four Gospels based on the chronology of the Fourth Gospel, it was possible to argue, and it was argued by "those who believed themselves entitled to speak in the name of criticism," that Tatian either did not know the Fourth Gospel, or did not value it.

If we had only possessed the apologetic writings of Tertullian, it might have been possible to argue that he also did not accept the Fourth Gospel. How absurd this would have been is only evident because we possess those writings which he addressed to Christians.

have been built and decorated at the end of the first century and the beginning of the second, the principal decorative motive is the vine. This certainly seems to suggest familiarity with the Fourth Gospel. If this is not considered sufficiently convincing because of the frequent use of the vine as a decorative motive in Pagan monuments, what is to be said of the painting which the vine decoration surmounts? This represents two persons partaking of the heavenly feast, the food on the table being bread and fish. As any one who knows anything about the symbolism of the paintings of the second century is aware, the mystic ideas underlying this scene must have been taken from a combination of the miracle of the loaves and fishes with the discourse in which Christ presented Himself as the bread of life. These ideas occur in the sixth chapter of the Fourth Gospel, but nowhere else in the New Testament. Traces of a picture of the Good Shepherd were also found by de Rossi in this vestibule and in another crypt close by. This is another clear link with the Fourth Gospel. The vestibule is the nucleus of the cemetery and it was built, as inscriptions show, by the Christian relations of Domitian probably between 90 and 96 before the persecution in his reign, when Flavius Clemens, the husband of Domitilla, was put to death, and Domitilla exiled. Under the floor of the vestibule de Rossi found coffins made of earthenware closed with tiles bearing the consular dates of the years 123 and 137.

In the narrow passage leading out of it loculi were found closed with tiles bearing stamps of the reigns of Antoninus Pius and Marcus Aurelius, but none later (*Bull. Arch. Christ.* for 1865, pp. 31–40 ; *Roma Sotterranea*, vol. i., p. 187).

Also in the Capella Græca in the Cemetery of Priscilla, which is attributed by the best authorities

to the early second century, there is a representation
of the raising of Lazarus and of the Eucharistic feast
in which latter the baskets of the miracle of the loaves
and fishes are shown on each side of the table, thus
connecting the ideas expressed in this picture in an
unmistakable manner with the sixth chapter of the
Gospel. Close to this chapel is the crypt of the Acilii
Glabriones, one of the most aristocratic families in
Rome, some of the members of which were Christians in
the first century (Marucchi, *Catacombe Romane*, p. 428).

This is quite sound archæological evidence that long
before the middle of the second century some of the
most characteristic teaching of the Fourth Gospel was
well known in Rome, so well known that the most
noble members of the Roman Church used representations of it to express their most cherished hopes and
to decorate their tombs. Canon Streeter has a theory
that the Gospel of Luke was written for the benefit
of the Roman Christian aristocracy, and especially for
T. Flavius Clemens, whom he supposes to have been
"Theophilus" (p. 539). This is quite possible, yet
in the ornamentation of the burial-place of the family
of Clemens we have evidence far stronger than conjecture that they turned to the Fourth Gospel and not
to that of Luke for symbols by means of which they
might express their faith and hope in Christ.

Does not the fact that such decoration exists in
the tombs of the most distinguished and best educated
Roman Christians show that those who had the best
opportunities of knowing the truth, and the most cogent
reasons for making sure about it, treated the Fourth
Gospel with at least as much respect as the other three
very soon after it was first published?

We pass on to consider Canon Streeter's treatment
of the evidence of Irenæus. First he reminds us that
there was in Asia, as we know from Papias, a person

named John who was commonly spoken of as the "disciple of the Lord." Therefore, when we find in Irenæus references to a disciple called " John " we must be cautious about drawing hasty conclusions. He then proceeds to re-tell the history of Irenæus.

We have, he says, no reason to suppose that Irenæus was born, or long resident, in Asia. He may have been at Smyrna only a few months. Here, no doubt, he heard Polycarp preach. "In the absence of any express statement to the effect, we are not entitled to infer that he was in any sense a pupil of Polycarp " (p. 443). If he heard references to " John," or even heard passages from the Gospel attributed to him read, how was a young boy to suppose that any one but the Apostle was meant ? " A boy's chronology is of the vaguest, and every grey-beard is a Methuselah." " Of course, had Irenæus continued to live in Asia, he must sooner or later have corrected such an impression. But if, after a short visit, he left for Gaul, HE WOULD HAVE FOUND NO ONE THERE ABLE TO CORRECT HIS ERROR." All this is very plausible IF certain quite unfounded assumptions are granted. IF Irenæus has given, as Canon Streeter hints, a grossly and deliberately exaggerated account of his connection with Polycarp ; IF he was only in Smyrna for a few months as an unsophisticated child, gazing with wide eyes at the venerable beard of the Methuselah-like bishop ; IF he went away from Asia immediately ; IF no one could have corrected his false impressions in Gaul, then this fanciful description of his early life might account for his subsequent mistakes.

First let us note that the imaginary picture here painted of Irenæus as a little boy on a casual visit to Smyrna, taken to church and listening—none too attentively—to the discourses of the venerable bishop, depends on nothing better than that faculty of

" creative memory " to which Canon Streeter ascribes some of the characteristic features of the Fourth Gospel, and the use of which (by the orthodox) he gently deprecates (p. 383). Let our readers turn to p. 14 of this book, where they will find the exact words in which Irenæus records his experience, and judge if Canon Streeter's version is a reasonable expansion of them. Secondly, let them examine the statement that if Irenæus had left Asia for Gaul after a short stay, he would have found no one in Gaul able to correct the error into which he is supposed to have fallen with regard to the identity of the person whom Polycarp referred to as " John." * On p. 71 of Canon Streeter's book we read : " The connection between Asia and the Church of Lyons, of which Irenæus was a member and ultimately bishop, was in no way peculiar to Irenæus himself. Eusebius preserves a letter written by the Churches of Lyons and Vienne to the Church of Ephesus —this implies a special affiliation of these Gallic Churches to the Church of Asia. It is therefore exceedingly probable that the Christianity of the Rhone valley was derived from Ephesus. In that case the text of the Gospels used there would naturally be the Ephesian text." Thus Canon Streeter himself supplies the proof that there was no reason why this supposed mistake of Irenæus about the identity of the " John " who wrote the Fourth Gospel should not have been corrected when he reached Gaul, since the connection between Gaul and Ephesus was so close.

* It should also be noted that in the letter to Florinus Irenæus appeals to his recollections of Polycarp as well as to his own. Florinus was obviously older than Irenæus, as it is said that he was trying to gain the approbation of Polycarp which could hardly be said of a boy. In any case this letter is virtually based on the recollections of both Irenæus and Florinus, for in such a letter Irenæus would hardly appeal to memories which Florinus would be in a position to denounce as false.

Next it is suggested (p. 445) that since Irenæus had in his boyhood made this confusion between the true author of the Gospel and the Apostle, he deliberately continued to believe it, as he was under the strongest temptation to do so. "Thus his evidence is not that of an impartial, nor, it would appear, of an exceptionally well-informed witness" (p. 445).

He is not impartial, because the main argument of his apologetic work depended on the supposed fact that the tradition of the great Churches was guaranteed to be true, because they had apostolic founders. He is not well-informed, because Canon Streeter, by some special intuition, knows that he was probably in Asia for only a short time and that he was far too young to understand what he heard there.

In short, his testimony is so worthless that Canon Streeter prefers to it that of a fourth-century hagiographer and that of a romancer of about the same date.

Irenæus says that Polycarp received his appointment in Asia from Apostles as bishop of the Church in Smyrna. But Pionius, the hagiographer above mentioned, attributes Polycarp's appointment to Bucolus, and the *Apostolic Constitutions* apparently date his episcopate after 100, that is, after the death of John.

It does not matter if Tertullian makes the same statement about Polycarp as Irenæus does. He is probably only copying Irenæus (p. 445).

If Canon Streeter's former arguments had done anything to weaken the force of the testimony of Irenæus, these additional supposed proofs of his fallibility might have some value in giving it the *coup de grâce*. We do not think, however, that he has contributed anything but the assumptions of a very vivid imagination working on suggestions made by many earlier critics towards discrediting Irenæus.

Therefore, however inexplicable the omission of

the name of John by these late authors may be, it is
far from being decisive against almost contemporary
testimony of Irenæus.

With regard to Papias, Canon Streeter has what
seems to be a really novel suggestion to make. He
thinks that Papias used the Fourth Gospel, but quoted
it under the name of the " Memoirs of the Elder "
(p. 447). He states that Justin seems to quote Mark
under the title of the " Memoirs of Peter," and then
goes on to say : " but this was not the ordinary Roman
usage ; otherwise (such was the desire to attach
apostolic authority to books accepted as a canonical)
it would certainly have prevailed. But if at Ephesus
Mark was commonly known as the ' Memoirs of Peter,'
then ' Memoirs of the Elder ' is just the title by which
we should expect the Fourth Gospel to be known."

Now, Justin does not use the actual expression
" Memoirs of Peter," a fact which Canon Streeter
relegates to a foot-note and leaves in Greek ; according
to the common reading he uses the expression " his
Memoirs " after mentioning Peter.

It should also have been stated that Otto would
here read ἀπομνημονεύματα αὐτῶν,* that is, "their
Memoirs," i.e., the Memoirs of the Apostles, in order
to bring the passage into agreement with the general
usage of Justin. A passage of this kind, occurring
only once and then not containing the crucial phrase
" Memoirs of Peter," is poor evidence on which to
found the conjecture that this was the usual name for
Mark at Ephesus.

Let it be granted for the sake of argument, as Canon
Streeter so confidently asserts in his parenthesis, that
there was in the second century a settled determination
to find apostolic authors for all canonical books and

* *Dial.* 106.

that the name "Memoirs of Peter" had become attached to the Gospel of Mark at Ephesus, then it will be found difficult to explain why it ever lost this name. On p. 559 of his book Canon Streeter gives his own explanation of how it came about that the Second Gospel does not bear the name of Peter at the present day. This explanation will only be cogent to those who accept some of his other theories.

Lastly, let us examine the curious syllogism : if the Gospel of Mark was called the "Memoirs of Peter" at Ephesus, the Fourth Gospel would be likely to be called the "Memoirs of the Elder" there. We should have thought that the obvious conclusion from this would have been that the Fourth Gospel would naturally be called the "Memoirs of John" there. We are told on p. 432 that the author of the Fourth Gospel stood to the Beloved Disciple in the same relationship in which Mark stood to Peter.

If it was natural that Mark's Gospel should be called after Mark's teacher at Ephesus, why should not the Elder's Gospel have been called by the name of his teacher by a generation which is supposed to have valued apostolic authorship above everything else ?

Canon Streeter then goes on to argue that, assuming an early and abiding confusion in the mind of Irenæus between the Apostle and the Elder, that simple-minded writer would be sure to try to reconcile all statements which he found in Papias about John with what he had heard from Polycarp. We know that Irenæus accepted the Second Epistle of John as being the work of the Apostle, and, since in that book the writer calls himself "the Elder," it would be natural for Irenæus to assume that this was an alternative title for the Apostle. If, therefore, he found a passage from the Fourth Gospel quoted by Papias as being from the "Memoirs of the Elder," he would consider this only what was to be expected (p. 448).

A quotation from Eusebius is employed to support this argument. He states (*Hist. Ecc.*, **v.** 8) that in a certain work " presumably now lost " Irenæus mentions the Memoirs of a certain apostolic Elder. A translation of the whole passage from Eusebius is given below : after mentioning the comments that Irenæus makes on certain of the books of the New Testament, Eusebius goes on to say that he also quoted the Wisdom of Solomon, and then says : " He also mentions the Memoirs of a certain apostolic Elder, whose name he has passed over in silence ; he also adds his expositions of the Sacred Scriptures. He, moreover, makes mention of Justin Martyr and Ignatius, taking some testimony also from the works written by these."

Since there are several references to the sayings of this unnamed Elder in the works of Irenæus which we possess, it does not seem absolutely necessary to suggest, as Canon Streeter does, that Eusebius is referring to some other work, now lost.

However, he really should have finished the quotation and given it in its context. Eusebius, having finished what he has to say about the comments that Irenæus made on the Gospels and the rest of the New Testament, passes on to the use that he made of the Wisdom of Solomon and the writers of his own time. Surely the natural inference from the order in which he mentions the authors is that the unnamed " Elder " is not to be classed among the writers of the New Testament, but among the early Ecclesiastical writers. Moreover, does any one think it probable that John the Elder wrote " expositions of the Sacred Scriptures," by which there is great probability that the Old Testament alone is meant ? It is generally believed that the unnamed Elder mentioned by Irenæus was Pothinus,

his predecessor in the see of Lyons, who was put to
death at the age of 90 and might well be called " an
apostolic Elder." Any one who refers to *Adv. Hær.*
iv. 27 will see the kind of reference which Irenæus
makes to this Elder.

Again, supposing that Papias did refer to the Fourth
Gospel as the " Memoirs of the Elder " and actually
quoted some words from it under this name, what
must Eusebius have thought of it ?

He was quite convinced by the long-standing tradition of the Church that the Fourth Gospel was written
by the son of Zebedee, and surely if he had found
Papias quoting it under the name of the " Memoirs
of the Elder " it must have attracted his attention.

He had himself discovered the existence of the
" Elder," and he was delighted with his discovery.
We might say, if we pleased, that he was not " an
impartial, nor, it would appear, an exceptionally
well-informed witness," for he can bring forward no
other evidence for the existence of the " Elder."

He must have looked for such other evidence : and
here it was ready to his hand. Why did he not
mention it ?

Canon Streeter has foreseen this objection and has
his answer to it ready. Eusebius had such a poor
opinion of the capacity of Papias, that he would
have considered even such an apparent blunder as
this " quite in keeping with his usual stupidity "
(p. 449).

Now, our belief in the very existence of " John the
Elder " depends on the credit that we give to the
intelligence of Papias.

If, after reading all his writings, Eusebius really
considered him such a hopeless simpleton as this, his
credit is gone for ever. So those " learned apologists,"
Provost Salmon and Dom Chapman, were perhaps

not so far wrong after all in their hesitation to find
two Johns in the famous passage (p. 450).

There can be only three explanations of the way
in which Eusebius treats the evidence of Papias, if he
found that Papias quoted passages from the Gospel
as being from the " Memoirs of the Elder," and that
he also stated that the Apostle John was put to death
by the Jews, as Canon Streeter henceforth always
assumes.

One is that given by Canon Streeter. Eusebius considered Papias such a thoroughly stupid person that his
evidence was of no value at all, even in matters where
it was quite clear and unambiguous. A second is that
Eusebius was as dull as Papias, and did not see what he
meant. A third explanation is that favoured by some
very drastic critics, such as Dr. Latimer Jackson, that
Eusebius, with a prudent regard of consequences to
Church tradition, passed over all the awkward parts
of the information he got from Papias about the
" Elder " and his works and only published those parts
of it which were favourable to his own theories about
the authorship of the Gospel and Apocalypse. This
method of partial quotation of awkward matter is
not unknown at the present day in " critical " literature,
and we have drawn attention to it several times in
the course of the first dissertation in this book. Those
who will may attribute this kind of thing to Eusebius,
but they have to explain how it is that no one ever
corrected him, if the matter was so open and obvious
in the works of Papias as Canon Streeter supposes.

If Canon Streeter's own explanation of " the silence
of Eusebius " is the true one, it will follow that he has
once more cut the ground from under his own feet.
He has successfully proved that the writer on whose
testimony the very existence of his supposed Evangelist
depends was regarded by those who knew the whole

of his writings as being an author the value of whose statements was quite negligible, or he has shown that the writer whose sagacity discovered the existence of the " Elder " was either as dull as, or duller than, Papias himself, or a singularly untrustworthy historian in his treatment of all other matters pertaining to this important question.

This is, however, the sad fate of all Ecclesiastical writers who dare to contradict, or seem to contradict, the main dogma of the critical school.

Polycrates is contemptuously dismissed as " hardly an unbiassed witness." With regard to the others, as we have seen, Polycarp was, at best, misunderstood ; Papias was such a blockhead that Eusebius could think him capable of writing any obvious absurdity ; Irenæus was a thoughtless child who misrepresented the experiences of his early years and clung to his mistakes through prejudice when he was grown up and in a position of great responsibility ; Tertullian copied his mistakes without inquiry or intelligence ; Justin, " like a modern apologist," wrote as he did in the hope of pleasing the obscurantists of his day ; Eusebius was either so dull or so dishonest that he only unravelled the tangled question of the authorship of the " Johannine literature " as far as suited his theories about the authorship of the Apocalypse, although he had the clue in his hand—the truth told by poor stupid Papias about the existence of the " Elder," his authorship of the Gospel, and the early death of the Apostle John in Palestine.

If the early Fathers of the Church were such men as the exigencies of this modern theory require us to believe—prejudiced, credulous and inclined only to accept and try to understand what fell in with their own expectations and desires—there was indeed great need that some man more capable than they should

be " raised up " to enable the Church to emerge from
the chrysalis of Jewish Apocalyptic and to conquer
the Græco-Roman world (p. 465).

The Church, we are told (p. 466), had no home base,
no collection of books specifically Christian, no coherently thought-out theology, and very little in the
way of organisation at the end of the first century.

We used to be allowed to think that, even if
Jerusalem had been destroyed, still there existed
Churches like Antioch, Rome and Ephesus, which had
been founded by Apostles and in which apostolic tradition was remembered and maintained. Now we learn
that, as far at least as Ephesus is concerned, this is a
figment of the confused brain of Irenæus. With regard
to Rome, Canon Streeter seems rather inclined to accept
some of the wild theories of Prof. Merrill (p. 490). It
seems to be allowed that Antioch produced, or at
least gave the weight of its authority to, the Gospel of
Matthew, which, of course, had not much connection
with the Apostle.

We also used to be taught to believe that even if
the Canon, as we now know it, had not been formulated,
still most of the books that constitute it were in existence and held in high honour for good and sufficient
reasons. It used to be generally allowed that St. Paul
had laid the foundations of a theology which, if not
" coherently thought-out," still served as a bond of
union between the Churches and was used by all
writers alike as being of considerable authority.

However, it now appears that the Christian Church
owes its preservation and subsequent success to the
fact that John the Elder was a Jew (p. 467). Not
necessarily a Jew of Palestine (p. 403), but still probably the last Jew to be the dominating spirit in a great
Gentile Church and a Jew of great personal gifts.
The fact that he had seen the Lord (at the age of

twelve ?) gave him "an authority all but apostolic."
While remaining true to his Jewish conceptions of the
unity and personality of God, he was able to write a
Gospel "intellectually acceptable to the Greek mind."

It is naturally objected that John the Elder is a
very shadowy figure to have this extraordinary and
decisive rôle in the history of religion and philosophy
thrust upon him.

But, says our author, "there are very few characters
in history who would not become shadowy if all their
writings were assigned to some one else and all the
information available about their character and career
was supposed to refer to some other person" (p. 467).

As a general statement this must, of course, be
accepted ; but in the case before us it is begging the
whole question to try to make a figure of flesh and blood
out of the "Elder" by attributing to him the writings
which the whole Church has until lately attributed to
the Apostle, not to mention the stories which later
Church writers tell of the Apostle, but which Canon
Streeter would transfer to the "Elder." What has
to be explained is the undoubted fact that, if the
"Elder" was really the author of the Fourth Gospel,
one of the greatest religious and dramatic geniuses
that the world ever produced did not leave an unmistakable trace of his existence in the records of his own
or any subsequent generation, until he was discovered
in an ambiguous fragment of a historian whom Canon
Streeter has shown to his own satisfaction to have been
one of the stupidest of writers in the opinion of those
who had the whole of his works (p. 449).

Those critics who reject the traditional account of
the authorship of the Fourth Gospel set themselves
the problem of trying to find a suitable author for it
from internal evidence.

All the Apostles are ruled out before the inquiry

opens. However, the external evidence that the
Gospel was written by a man named " John " is so
strong and so harmless, in itself, to the general
position taken up with regard to the Gospels by the
critical school, that it is generally accepted without
hesitation. The fact that it is possible to extract
from the well-known passage in Papias that there may
have been a " John " in Asia who was not the Apostle,
is a veritable godsend to these critics in search of an
author. Some of them are quite satisfied with the
supposed " Elder " as an author of the Gospel, others
imagine that it was written by another " John," possibly a pupil of his, or a whole school of pupils. Some
require a " John the Seer " in addition. And so it
goes on—as many " Johns " are provided as may be
required by the taste and fancy of the critic.

We submit, however, that they are all rather
shadowy persons. The statement that John the Elder
was a Jew, which is the only piece of information
that Canon Streeter can give us with any confidence
about him, seems to be founded on the following
syllogism :

John the Elder wrote the Fourth Gospel.

The man who wrote the Fourth Gospel was a Jew.

Therefore John the Elder was a Jew.
But many critics dispute the major premise, and
many dispute the minor, so that, critically speaking,
the conclusion is somewhat uncertain, and the poor
" Elder " remains rather shadowy.

He is, in fact, such a shadowy figure that, when
Canon Streeter wishes to give us more information
about him in addition to that which has already been
mentioned, he is compelled to write as follows :
" For the rest of this chapter I permit myself to stray
from the paths of stern historical method, and, in the
absence of determinative evidence, allow the historical

imagination to wander freely in the pasture-land of speculation " (p. 468).

The Fourth Gospel, in spite of the prestige of its author, who was known to have seen the Lord Himself, was too startling a novelty to be received without question, especially when the matter which it contained was written down and began to get into the hands of the country clergy. Old-fashioned Church members regarded it as the " thin end of the wedge " ; the country clergy accused the author of " selling the pass to the Church's enemies " (p. 471) ; the working classes who could understand nothing but " Hell-fire and the Immediate Coming with an exact date given " (p. 479) were in danger of being alienated. It, however, attracted the bright young presbyters who had grasped the New Theology.

In a word, it fulfilled in its own time that desideratum of which we hear so much to-day—it restated the Gospel in the terms of the Modern Mind. It introduced the novel and " unapostolic " * term LOGOS. It interpreted the Second Coming in a spiritual sense without " absolutely denying an Apocalyptic Judgment." Again, " for all practical purposes it substitutes the Coming of the Comforter for the visible Return of Christ." " It made Christianity a possible religion for the educated Greek," and " intellectually respectable " (pp. 468–481 *passim*).

As all this avowedly belongs to the realm of fantasy, we will leave it to the judgment of our readers, only asking them to refer to John v. 28, 29, xii. 48, and 1 John ii. 18, 28. With regard to the first of these quotations, Canon Streeter has already on p. 382 (following Loisy, Scholten and other critics) suggested that it is an editorial interpolation.† He seems to have

---

* Notice the question-begging nature of this epithet.

† Dean Inge apparently accepts this verse as genuine.

made no comment on the other verses. In the part of the book in which he makes this suggestion he is presumably following the " stern historical method," so common in " critical " works, of making a theory first and then rejecting from the text of the author on whom the comment is being made everything that does not agree with it.

The Gospel, then, was received by the more advanced circles in the Church of Asia as providing a welcome relief in the face of the intellectual difficulties of the time, but the moderates regarded it " without enthusiasm."

Canon Streeter considers that the incident of which a record is preserved in the Third Epistle of John had to do with the dislike of the country bishops for the rationalism of John the Elder (p. 471).

Diotrephes was an old-fashioned Christian who resented the presence in his diocese of some of the " bright young presbyters " who were sent by John to teach his " New Theology " which the Bishop regarded as dangerously akin to Gnosticism. On this we have only to remark that the epithet translated "who loveth to have the pre-eminence" (ὁ φιλοπρωτεύων) is a strange one to apply to a lawfully constituted Bishop, especially if he were an old man.

Canon Streeter, still in the realm of speculation, now passes on to consider the meaning and purpose of the last chapter of the Gospel. He turns with unexpected severity on some of his fellow-critics (such as Loisy and Bacon) with regard to this chapter.

" All those (theories) which do not begin by recognising that the chapter is a work of genius may be dismissed. Critics who have bemused their faculties by the study of one another's theories so far as to think that any purely mechanical editing or any pettifogging controversial motive has here found expression need not be listened to. The style of the added conclusion to Mark is pedestrian : the Appendix to John is great literature " (p. 471).

We are glad to be able for once to agree heartily with our author's opinion.

The chapter is clearly an afterthought. Was it added by another hand ? The style and gift of imaginative description suggest the same master-mind that conceived and wrote the Gospel. Yet there are certain minutiæ of diction that point to another hand. Still, if it be by a pupil, it was written by one " saturated with his master's spirit " (p. 472). It is strange to note how even here, where it is most vital to the argument now to be developed, Canon Streeter still desires to be in the van of " progress " and shrinks back from even such semi-orthodoxy as the supposition that the last chapter was by the same author as the rest of the Gospel.

Why, then, was this chapter added ? Certainly for no unimportant reason. It must have been added to meet some vital need of the Church of those days. It is supposed that the thinking men of the generation when the Gospel was written were much perplexed when they saw one Apostle after another die off without there being any sign of the Return of the Lord. Mark ix. 1 was a great stumbling-block to them. Even the " Elder " is thought to have been troubled by this difficulty, especially when his master the " Beloved Disciple " was taken away.

Canon Streeter apparently allows (p. 433) that there was some tradition in the Church that this disciple at least should survive until the Second Coming, and his death upset the " Elder " very much. So, being a mystic, he managed to " slip into a mystic trance " in which it was revealed to him that what the Lord had really said to the Apostle was not, " He shall tarry till I come," but, " If I will that he tarry—what is that to thee ? " (p. 478).

This had satisfied his own mind at the time. He had worked out a new view according to which no visible return of Christ upon the earth was to be looked for, but only His spiritual presence as the Comforter. He also inserted in his Gospel discourses (p. 372) which he invented (possibly also in a convenient trance) and put them into the mouth of Christ to give His authority to his own views.*

But now a new crisis had arisen in the Church after the Gospel had been finished. The persecution of Domitian had revived Apocalyptic ideas. " John the Seer " wrote the Apocalypse. Men's minds were again turned to the prophecies of Christ in Mark, and Matthew was beginning to be known. The only hope of the fulfilment of Mark ix. 1 now centred in the " Elder," the last survivor of " those that had seen the Lord." What was he to do ? " Long ago he had made up his mind that Christ's prophecy of an immediate coming bore another interpretation and

---

* Yet on p. 388 Canon Streeter says : " It would seem to follow that John could not, consistently with his purpose, have recorded as history any incident which he did not believe himself to have actually occurred." We can only suppose that, according to Canon Streeter's ideas, he was so bemused with visions, as is suggested on p. 390, that he mistook what he saw in his visions for facts.

This is also the view of Loisy. Yet on p. 406, Canon Streeter suggests that the " Elder " attempted to conjecture the names of the disciples that visited the empty tomb, and on p. 390 he says that the " Elder " knew of a story about an interview between Christ and a Samaritan woman, " which, no doubt, to some extent he re-wrote." These two supposed instances of the " Elder's " literary activity do not seem much like innocent, if weak-minded, bemusement with visions. Surely the more straightforward explanation, on the critical basis, of these passages is to say, as the Canon does on p. 417, that " John's main purpose in writing was doctrinal and not historical." Or to say with Réville : " In the circles where the Fourth Gospel was written historic reality had not the least value."

that no visible Return was to be looked for " (p. 477). But how was he to help the deluded multitude worked into a frenzy of expectation by the prophecies of " John the Seer " ?

He would compose a supplement to his Gospel (or perhaps a pupil composed it for him after he was dead) in which he would attain three ends :

(1) He would give confirmation to the story of the meeting with the disciples in Galilee after the Resurrection, which is imagined to have existed in the lost ending of Mark (p. 473).

(2) He would work his trance into an historical form and by this means make it clear to the simpler members of the Church that Christ never promised that any of the Apostles should tarry till He came (p. 480).

(3) He would repeat in the most impressive manner, as his last word to his followers, the command of Christ to feed the lambs of the flock, which may have also stood in the lost ending of Mark which is supposed to have been known at Ephesus (p. 480). It was not enough that these words should be found in Mark— " that was the old-fashioned Gospel now."

He himself, the leader of the Modernists, even if " something of the old fogey," would write down these words, lest his bright young presbyters should forget that they had a duty towards the ignorant multitude with their out-of-date ideas and their incapacity to appreciate his restatement of the fundamentals of Christianity.

We really do not know what to say about all this. From one point of view it speaks for itself. We used to be taught a method of proving geometrical problems which consisted in assuming that the thing to be proved was not true and then tracing out the absurdities that followed from this supposition. We have, we fear, wearied our readers by this long summary of Canon

H

Streeter's " wanderings in the pasture-land of speculation." This much good, however, may spring from
our review : if these are the results which a man of
great learning and remarkable ingenuity draws from
supposing that the Fourth Gospel had not an apostolic
author, is there not a strong probability that his
original supposition was mistaken ? To us at least
the paradoxical conclusions to which he comes seem
like a proof by *reductio ad absurdum* that the Gospel
had an apostolic author.*

It is interesting to compare with these wild theories
the sober account of the origin of the Gospel given by
the late Canon Scott Holland in his book on the Fourth
Gospel.

We know, of course, that there was in the early
Church a strong expectation of the immediate return
of Christ, and we also know that this expectation
gradually faded away under the discipline of experience. We can trace the process in the Pauline
Epistles from the expectation in Thessalonians that
the Apostle might be among those who were alive and
remained to his quiet anticipation of immediate death
in Second Timothy. We shall, of course, be reminded
that this is probably not genuine, but at any rate it
reflects what men of those days thought the Apostle
ought to feel.

Then, again, the writer of Second Peter calmly
confronts the mockers who said : " Where is the
promise of his coming ? " in the manner of a Hebrew
prophet, with the reminder that God's ways are not as
man's ways. This is the way in which the difficulty
was faced as a matter of fact, as far as the evidence goes.

* The germ of all these ideas is stated in a crude way by Renan.
" Chaque retard que Jésus mettait à venir était un pas de plus vers
sa divinisation : et cela est vrai que c'est juste à l'heure où le dernier
rêve millenaire disparait que la divinité de Jésus se proclame d'une
manière absolue." (*Vie de Jésus*, p. 481).

There is no evidence whatever that the Gospel was ever considered to be an apologetic work of the kind that Canon Streeter supposes. If we regard the last chapter of the Gospel as an account of something that really happened, told by one of those who were present, the story presents no difficulty at all, at least to those who are prepared to admit that Christ was a supernatural Being and did rise from the dead. The author added it to his Gospel to correct a misunderstanding about himself which had arisen from misquotation of a saying of Christ. The meaning of this saying, even when correctly reported, was such that it could only be interpreted rightly by the course of events.

When the aged Apostle felt that his end was near, he became sure that Christ had not promised that he should tarry until His second coming, and he wished to make this clear.

Canon Streeter says that this last chapter of the Gospel is great literature and that the writer of it was a genius ; as he supposes that it is little better than a piece of imaginative dramatisation he is quite justified in holding these opinions.

Could Shakespeare himself, if provided with the Synoptic account of Peter and John, have written anything more dramatically convincing than the portrait of Peter, first needing the insight of John to perceive that the Figure on the shore was the Lord, and then jumping into the sea in order to get to Him first, yet afterwards not forgetting his duty as a fisherman in hauling the net to land ? What could be more in keeping with his portrait in the Synoptists than his eagerness once more to confess his love to his Master, and his disappointment because his confession was not at once accepted ?

Let us, moreover, observe the skill (on the supposition that the whole story is a dramatic fiction) with which Peter's tendency to ask unnecessary and somewhat presumptuous questions is made use of to lead up to the crucial point of the story—the introduction of the true explanation of the saying that "that disciple should not die."

All this is indeed the work of a genius. But what are we to say of the portrait of the risen Christ—so dignified, so loving yet so exacting in His demands on His erring disciple, and so firm in checking his ill-timed curiosity? Could "John the Elder," or any one else of that age, have invented that?

We prefer to believe, in spite of the fact that Loisy finds much in this chapter "d'une puérilité enfantine," that we have here to do with true history written by one who had, in no artificial sense of the words, actually "seen the Lord." We do not envy the state of mind of those who are content to regard such a passage as this as nothing better than material for the literary dissecting table.

* * * * *

A "short and easy way" of disproving the historical character of the Fourth Gospel is to be found with curious unanimity at the beginning of many modern discussions of the subject.

Dean Inge, in his article in *Cambridge Biblical Essays*, states this opinion as follows: "We have before us a composition which does not pretend to conform to the modern standard of history or biography, but which does claim to be a true interpretation of the person and work of Christ, an elucidation of the inner spirit of the new religion addressed to the Christian Church about 100 years after the birth of Christ. The Evangelist no more wishes us to believe that Jesus spoke all the words which he puts into His mouth than that He spoke Greek. . . . The whole book is a free composition by the writer himself, inspired, as he believed, and as we have every reason to believe, by the Spirit of Jesus. Its value does not depend on apostolic authorship, or on written traditions reaching back to Galilee. The discourses bear primarily on the conditions of Christian life in A.D. 100. The Fourth Gospel is more of a theological treatise than a biography and more of an apologia than a theological treatise."

Dr. Brooke, in the same collection of essays, says : " A Gospel is not a history. It is not even a biography. It may, or may not, contain true history : it makes no claim to completeness of historical presentation. What the writer says, or leaves unsaid, is determined by the object with which he writes, and the object is to provide Christians and others who are interested in Christianity with adequate instruction about the facts of the life of Jesus of Nazareth and the contents of His teaching, to enable them to form true opinions about what He was and what He did, and to mould their lives accordingly as worthy members of the Christian society which the Christians to whom the Evangelist addressed himself believed Him to have founded." This, he says, is clearly stated in the prologue of St. Luke and more clearly still by St. John, and is also implied in the first few lines of the other Gospels. " The Gospel makers had to give a more permanent form to the Gospel, and the Gospel was the whole message of the Christ—what He taught and did and was." " It was complete, but not a history, or a biography " (p. 292).

Canon Streeter states (p. 365) that Mark and Luke depart little from the literary model of the day in which they lived, " but the Fourth Gospel stands apart. It does not purport to be a life of Christ. Avowedly it is a selection for a special purpose." . . . " It belongs neither to history nor to biography, but to the library of devotion."

With regard to the statements of these writers, we have to say that Dean Inge begins his description very well, but there seems to be something hidden under the apparently harmless expression that the Gospel " does not pretend to conform to the modern standard of history, or biography," for he goes on to say that the whole book is a " free composition by the writer himself " and apparently has little historical value. Why we should have " every reason to believe " that the Spirit of Jesus inspired a work of this kind, and why it does not matter whether the book was written by an Apostle, he does not attempt to explain. The rest of the passage consists of unsupported assertions.

Dr. Brooke's statement is mostly made up of truisms, but why does he say that a Gospel, being such as he has defined it to be, is neither history nor biography ? He cannot mean that in order to be called a history or biography a book must necessarily contain all the facts about the life of a man. This is obviously impossible in any case. Like any other writer, the author of a Gospel must select his facts, and even if he selects them for an edifying purpose, this does not seem to be any reason why his work should not be a history or biography in the ordinary sense of these words, provided that the facts that he sets down are true.

The supposition lying behind this confused statement seems to be that the Gospels, like some of the lives of the Saints, were written simply with a view to edification, without much regard being paid to the historical truth of the statements that they contain.

This is certainly the opinion of certain Continental critics even with regard to the Synoptic Gospels, as may be seen from the following quotations.

Jülicher writes: "What the Evangelists know and tell is a mixture of truth and poetry. . . . Their object is not to understand or to appreciate the Jesus of History, but to believe in Him and to love Him before all things and to teach men to hope in Him. They do not describe the Jesus of real life, but Christ as He appeared in the hearts of those that believed in Him" (*Einleitung in das N.T.*, pp. 290, 293).

And Loisy writes: "It is because the Gospels are before all things books of edification that their authors do not fear to treat the traditional matter with a liberty which renders quite useless all the artifices by means of which a certain type of exegesis tries to disguise it" (*Autour d'un petit livre*, p. 44).

We now come to Canon Streeter. He admits that the Gospels of Mark and Luke depart little from the standard of biography of the time when they were written—how little even this statement admits their historical trustworthiness may be seen from the treatment that they receive in the rest of his book—" but the Fourth Gospel does not even purport to be a life of Christ." Why? Because it is a selection for a special purpose and "belongs neither to history nor to biography, but to the library of devotion." This seems in no way to follow from the premises, unless we assume that the edifying lessons which the Fourth Gospel was designed to teach cannot have been based on any acts or words of Jesus, but are only symbolic descriptions and amplifications of the thoughts and feelings of those who had come to believe, we know not how, that Jesus of Nazareth was the Christ in a sense far transcending not only what the Jews expected from their Messiah, but also any claims that Jesus ever made for Himself.

This is to assume the point at issue. Moreover, this theory of the character of the Gospel obliges us to believe that the thoughts of men about Christ are greater, more ennobling and more potent for good, than the thoughts of Christ about Himself, for it is admitted by Canon Streeter that the Fourth Gospel was the book that made it possible for Christianity to become the religion of the educated classes among the Greeks and saved it from remaining an obscure Jewish sect.

The fact that the author of the Fourth Gospel wrote his book with the avowed object of inducing men to believe that Jesus was the Son of God can no more *ipso facto* prove that his book is not historic than the fact that Lord Macaulay wrote his history to glorify the Whig Revolution of 1688 can prove by itself that his book is not historic. The only possible way in which such a statement can be proved is by examining the book in detail and showing how far, if at all, the supposed purpose of the author has interfered with his presentation of historical facts.

This is, however, not done now. Attempts to do it have often been made in the past and have been answered. The writers mentioned above assume that they have proved their case by merely stating it and then go on their way with some such airy remark as that of Dean Inge * that, as the conversations with Nicodemus and the Samaritan woman, where no witnesses were present, can hardly be historical, presumably one can think what one pleases about the historical character of the rest.

Another " short way " of disparaging the historical character of the Fourth Gospel by endeavouring to deprive it of an apostolic author is to argue that it could not possibly have been written by a Galilean fisherman whom his contemporaries regarded as being " unlearned and ignorant." It is also objected by a

* Following Renan, *Vie de Jésus*, pp. 490, 494.

recent writer on the subject that the " Son of Thunder "
who wanted to call down fire from heaven on a
Samaritan village that would not receive our Lord
could not have written the words, " Little children, love
one another." There is not much force in the latter
objection for those who believe that Christianity has
any power to change the character. As for the first
objection, it cannot be said to be a full statement of
the case.

There seems to be three possible aspects under
which the author of the Gospel may be regarded.

(1) He was an unknown religious genius belonging
to the second generation of Christians, a mystic and a
visionary, who evolved the Gospel out of his own
religious experience and that of his contemporaries.
To quote the words of Dean Inge, " The discourses
bear primarily on the condition of Christian life in
A.D. 100." Or to quote Canon Streeter, " The doctrine
propounded in these discourses . . . was organically related to what Christ taught in such a way as to be the
doctrine which Christ would have taught, had He
been explicitly dealing with the problems confronting
the Church at the time when the Gospel was written "
(op. cit., p. 371).

It is allowed that the subject-matter of the Gospel
has some ill-defined basis in fact and tradition, but it
is thought that most of the details in which both the
discourses and the events on which they are made to
depend differ from the Synoptists were either invented
by the author, or came to him in some state of ecstasy
in which he could not distinguish fact from vision.
His work was in some way or other related to the
later Epistles of St. Paul. In him, to use the words
of Harnack (Hist. Dog. I. 96–98), " A Pauline Christ
walks the earth, far more human than the Christ of
Paul, yet far more divine."

Professor Gardner says in the *Cambridge Biblical Essays*, pp. 382, 394, that the Christianity of Paul was not only different from, but contrasted with that of the Synoptic writers. "This fact, long concealed from Christian readers by the supposition that the Fourth Gospel was wholly the work of a companion of Jesus and of great historical value, is now patent to every critical student of the New Testament. The theology of the Fourth Gospel, though not wholly Pauline, is post-Pauline. Without the work of Paul it could not have come into existence in its present shape." The more devout holders of this view add that the author of the Fourth Gospel was undoubtedly influenced in his visions and writings by the Holy Spirit, and that his portrait of Christ, although unhistorical, is not necessarily false.

(2) He was in some sense a follower of Christ and an eyewitness of most, if not of all, the events which he records. We have seen how Canon Streeter tries to combine these two views and how he endeavours to cut down the personal contact between the Evangelist and Christ to the narrowest possible limits.

(3) He was one of the Twelve. If this be granted, probably every one would admit that he must have been the Apostle John. It may be allowed that he was not an educated man in the sense that St. Paul was, but it does not therefore follow that he was illiterate still less that he may not have been a man of genius. Canon Streeter is obliged to suppose that his imaginary "Elder" was a man who transcended "the category of development in the slow biological sense of the term," and he can hardly refuse us the right to make the same supposition about John the Apostle who, as he has demonstrated, was the only one of the Twelve whom we can believe to have been the Beloved Disciple.

It must also be remembered that the traditional view of the authorship does not so imperatively demand a genius for the author as the critical view. All that the traditional view demands is that the author should have been of such a disposition as to be able to comprehend more sympathetically and to remember more faithfully some of our Lord's deeper sayings than the other disciples. If this view is taken, the real and original greatness of the Gospel stands to the credit of the Master, and only the selection and arrangement, and, to a certain extent, the diction, to the credit of the disciple.

Moreover, the traditional theory also gives some explanation of the anti-Jewish tone which is to be found in the Gospel and of the philosophical character of the prologue and of some of the wording of the discourses, for it allows that the author, after suffering much at the hands of his countrymen, went to live in a famous Greek city which was also a centre of philosophic thought.

Besides this, many still believe, with some support from exponents of the most recent theories, that the writer of the Gospel was inspired for the work that he had to do. In any case it is certain either that our Lord did promise some such supernatural assistance to His followers, or that the Fourth Evangelist put this promise into His mouth in order to pass off his imaginations or visions as authoritative.

The present fashion among those who endeavour to write lives of Christ is to treat the Synoptists as the only reliable authorities and to point out that there is quite enough in them to afford a basis for the Catholic faith. This may be granted ; in point of fact the Church existed and flourished for many years before the Fourth Gospel was written. It must, however, be remembered that there was something else behind

the faith of the Church in the first century besides the
matter contained in the Synoptists. There was the
oral teaching of the Apostles. What this was like we
may perhaps be allowed to conjecture from the acknowledged Epistles of St. Paul, the First Epistle of St.
Peter, and the Acts of the Apostles. St. Paul expressly
tells us that he compared his teaching with that of
the Twelve and that as a result of this he was given
" the right hand of fellowship." It is on record that
on certain points touching the observance and value
of the Jewish Law his teaching differed much from
that of leaders of the Church at Jerusalem, but there
is not the slightest sign that his Christological teaching
differed in any way from theirs. Surely the Jewish
Christians would have been at least as sensitive with
regard to teaching that seemed to deny the unity of
God as they were about teaching which seemed to
disparage the ceremonial Law. We know that there
was a sect among the Jewish Christians that taught
that Jesus was a mere man, who received some special
gift of divine adoption at his baptism, but that sect
was always regarded as heretical, and there is no evidence that it received any encouragement from any
of the Twelve. Even if we are not allowed by some of
the latest lights of criticism to be too confident about
the authorship of the First Epistle of Peter, yet it
cannot be disputed that it is an early writing and that
whoever forged it would be obliged to insert in it only
such teaching as the people of those times considered
suitable to the general character of apostolic tradition.

As for the Acts, it is true that Canon Streeter will
not permit us to regard the speeches in it as repre-
senting what Peter and Paul actually said, but only
what Luke considered they ought to have said, still
he has to admit that these speeches may be taken as
representative of " pre-Pauline Gentile Christianity,"

that is, the result of primitive apostolic teaching on an intelligent Gentile mind.

Then there is the more developed Christology of the later Epistles of St. Paul and that of the Epistle to the Hebrews and the Apocalypse to be accounted for.*

We are told by one distinguished critic that the Synoptic portrait of Jesus is not a product of Church Theology, but survived in spite of it, and we are encouraged in every way to draw a decisive line between the teaching of the Synoptics and that of the rest of the New Testament, as, for example, by Professor Gardner who, as we have already seen, says that the Christianity of Paul is not only different from, but contrasted with, that of the Synoptic writers.

If even the early Epistles of St. Paul as well as the Fourth Gospel not only went beyond but also contradicted the simple teaching which was given by the first teachers of Christianity, who on this theory did not go outside " the Synoptic portrait of Jesus," it is remarkable that we have no record of any opposition to these writings arising in ultra-orthodox circles on the ground of their extravagant Christology. Canon Streeter has painted for us the situation which he supposes to have arisen when the Fourth Gospel was first published at Ephesus, where he represents the Church as having been only nourished up on the Gospel of Mark, with a possible later addition of the Gospels of Luke and Matthew. He has not told us how the Church was perturbed when it first received the Epistle to the Ephesians and that to the Colossians, which came to it before the Gospel of Mark was put into writing.

Surely by the time the Fourth Gospel was written the Church of Ephesus must have become used to theological shocks.

---

* Canon Scott Holland has dealt admirably with this topic in his book *The Fourth Gospel*.

If we are allowed to think that the Synoptic Gospels do not contain a complete account of the apostolic teaching, but that there was a further element in it of such a character as to form a reasonable basis for the Christological teaching of St. Paul, the Fourth Evangelist and the authors of the Epistle to the Hebrews and the Apocalypse, then the production, contents and reception of these books becomes reasonably explicable.

But if, on the other hand, we are compelled to believe that Christ was nothing more than the so-called " Jesus of History," produced by infinite labour and ingenuity by certain recent writers out of suitably edited and much curtailed versions of the Synoptists, then we still have to solve the problem, not only of how the Synoptic Gospels came to be what they are, but also how the rest of the New Testament came to be written, and, what is much more difficult to explain, how it came to be received.

Let us try to set out the supposed situation at some length. The original teachers of Christianity preached a Gospel which is to be found within the limits of the Gospel of Mark after it has been suitably edited in accordance with modern ideas, with the addition of such other traditions, now embodied in the other two Gospels, as do not offend against present-day conceptions of historical probability. A more exact definition of this supposed early Christian teaching is hardly possible, owing to the difference of opinion among the critics with regard to details.

Some such teaching, according to Canon Streeter, got even to Ephesus, where it was regarded as strict orthodoxy at the end of the first century ; so teaching of this kind must have been prevalent for many years and been widely spread.

According to some extreme exponents of this view,

the earliest preachers of Christianity did not teach that Jesus was a Saviour ; even this was an importation from later theological speculation and had a Greek rather than a Hebrew origin.

However this may be, it is certain that in a few years the whole of this simple teaching was perverted and overlaid by " Church theology " to such an extent that even the Synoptic narratives have become corrupted by it, and the rest of the books of the New Testament give us quite a false idea of what primitive Christianity really was. If we ask who was the author of this perversion, the only answer that the available information permits the critics to give is that it must have been in part, or altogether, the work of St. Paul.

We know that he taught a high soteriological and Christological doctrine, and some members of the modern school would have us believe that there was little or nothing in the original Christian teaching to warrant this. Some say that it was a legitimate development and some say that it was not, but none of them succeed in explaining how he got his writings received by the Church at large.

He was a man who had many enemies, especially at Jerusalem, which was not only the centre of the Christian world at that time, but also the source of the supposed uncontaminated Gospel. They found fault readily enough with some of his teaching, and even made him answer for it before a council, but his teaching about the saving power of Christ and the divinity of His Person seems to have been accepted without the slightest hesitation.

Even if we allow this school of critics to assume the existence of another genius who transcended the " category of development in the slow biological sense of the term," we should still find it impossible to admit that St. Paul could have written as he had done about Christ with no other antecedents than the " Jesus of History," certain apocalyptic ideas derived mostly from the Apocrypha, and a few suggestions from the Greek-Oriental mystery religions.*   But even if we did admit that this was possible, we should still expect to have explained to us how he managed to get his revolutionary ideas accepted without dispute or comment in all parts of the Christian world and how his teaching influenced the works of the Synoptists, when they reached their final form, to such an extent that it requires all the resources of the most modern critical surgery to rid them of the extraneous matter for which he is so largely responsible.

To persons of ordinary mentality who are not capable of these flights of imagination it seems about as likely that St. Paul could have got his teaching accepted by the leaders of the Church at Jerusalem as that Loisy could have got his writings on the Gospels accepted by the Roman hierarchy at the present day.

Unless we are prepared to admit that the teaching of the Apostles contained more than is set out in express terms in the Synoptic Gospels, we have still got to explain how St. Paul was ever allowed to be the official missionary to the Gentiles sent out by the Church of Jerusalem.   His Epistles are probably all earlier than the final redaction of any of the Synoptic Gospels, and it is plain from their form that his developed teaching was known and accepted in the places to which they were sent.

The truth seems to be that the Synoptic Gospels contained an account of the incidents in the life of Christ and of such parts of His teaching as were

* For a full treatment of this topic, see Machen's *Origin of Paul's Religion*.   (Hodder & Stoughton.)

considered most suitable for inquirers and catechumens, and that something more was taught to those who became full members of the Church. What this something was we may conjecture from the fact that, as far as we know, the Christological doctrine of the rest of the New Testament was generally received by the members of the Church when it was set out in the various books in which we now have it. There is no proof that even the " Alogoi " objected to the Christology of the Fourth Gospel.

Let us go back for a moment to the objection that a man like John the Apostle could not have produced such a book as the Fourth Gospel because of his lack of education and early prejudices.

If we may be allowed to assume that such a Person as the Jesus depicted in the Synoptists did actually exist, and by this we mean a Person such as is described by the Synoptists as they stand, without any editing or curtailment, who can measure the extent of the influence of His presence and words on a susceptible mind ? Does not this dispose of the argument that, although some better-educated follower of our Lord might have written the Fourth Gospel, John the fisherman could not have written it ?

If it be granted that one of the Twelve may have written the Gospel, is there not a strong probability that it may contain on the whole a reliable account of certain events in the life of Christ and of the discourses to which they give rise which have been omitted from the other Gospels ?

We must consider very carefully what probability there is that if Jesus is truly depicted for us in the Synoptic Gospels, and if the Acts gives us a reliable account of the way in which His followers regarded Him after the resurrection, any of them would have dared to invent incidents in His life and to put words

I

into His mouth " which he (the Evangelist) knew quite
well were not so delivered " (Streeter, *op. cit.*, p. 372).
This is obviously so improbable that the critics
devise all sorts of expedients to keep the author of
the Gospel and its Subject as far apart as possible.
The Tübingen School acted quite logically when it
endeavoured to prove that the Gospel was written by
a Gentile well on in the second century. Now that it
is universally admitted that this view is untenable—
and most critics allow that the author was at least
in immediate contact with the apostolic generation,
if not in some sense an eyewitness of the life of Christ—
the most desperate efforts are made, as we see from
Canon Streeter's book, to reduce the contact between
the author of the Gospel and Christ to the smallest
possible limits.

Still, the Gospel exists, and some one must have
written it before the end of the first decade of the
second century.

It is either a record of experience, influenced, no
doubt, by the author's personality, but still in the main
due to the action of another life on his, or else it is
chiefly an imaginary work, like the *Divina Commedia*
of Dante, with a certain basis of fact derived from
the Synoptists, a few floating traditions, and a " pilgrim's knowledge " of Jerusalem. The discourses are
imaginary, the incidents are mostly invented and
certainly much embellished. Their dramatic fitness
and their appropriateness to a Personality such as the
world has never seen before or since count for nothing,
or an attempt is made to account for them by the
ascription of unusual genius to the author, or of a
capacity to see such things in visions as no other man
ever saw.

It is necessary also to admit that the book was
almost universally accepted soon after it was written

both in the East and in the West, in spite of the difficulty of harmonising much of its contents with the already accepted accounts of the life and teaching of Christ. It is comparatively easy to account for this if it was well known that the author was the Beloved Disciple and the last survivor of the Twelve, but on the supposition that he was the " Elder " or some other man called " John " there is a good deal to be explained which never has been explained.

Certainly those who believe that the Gospel was really the creation of an Eastern mystic and at the same time are compelled to admit that it was not long before it was received by the whole Church as on an equality with the other three Gospels deserve the blessing that, according to one critical school, is the prerogative of the Beloved Disciple, for they believe something which they assuredly have never seen.

"Credo quia absurdum," said Tertullian; and he finds strange followers among some of our more imaginative modern writers.

* * * * *

The portrait of Socrates presented to us by Xenophon is thought by many to be paralleled in the case of the Gospels by the portrait of Christ presented to us by the Synoptists, while the portrait of Socrates presented to us by Plato is paralleled by that presented in the Fourth Gospel. At first sight this comparison seems to tell strongly in favour of the usual critical attitude towards this Gospel. Xenophon, the unimaginative and practical man of the world, gives us the truest representation of the historic Socrates, while Plato, the idealist and philosopher, uses Socrates as a mouthpiece for his own teaching and theories, which were really quite alien to the homely philosophy of the old dialectician.

There are, however, as many differences as parallels

between the cases. In the first place nothing depended on whether the readers of Plato's dialogues believed that Socrates uttered the words attributed to him, or not. They did not believe his arguments because Socrates was said to have employed them, but because they were led to them by a process of reasoning. The last thing that Socrates ever claimed to be was a messenger from heaven. When the Delphic Oracle declared that he was the wisest of men, he supposed that the only reason why that distinction was bestowed upon him was that he knew that he knew nothing at all. Nothing depended on his personality. If he had never lived, it would not have made the smallest difference to the credibility of the teaching of Plato. He is not even represented as the author of the myths which are given a sort of prophetic or oracular authority by being attributed to fabulous persons of ancient time. Plato was justified by the literary fashion of his day in putting his own developed doctrine in the mouth of his master. Every one understood his meaning.

Even here it must be remembered that we do not know how far the seed-thoughts of the Platonic philosophy may have been derived from Socrates. Xenophon may have failed to see more in Socrates than he has shown us in the *Memorabilia* because of the limited and practical nature of his mind. Plato with his immense potential poetic and philosophic power may have been inspired as a young man by his contact with the mind of Socrates and have felt that all his subsequent development was conditioned by this early influence. Such modesty is not uncommon in truly great minds that have come under an extraordinary influence that has caused their powers to fructify in a way that they never anticipated and led them to " voyage through strange seas of thought " with no spiritual companionship except the memory of the revered master of their youth. This is what we believe happened in the case of the author of the Fourth Gospel; but the parallel is not complete. Everything in the philosophy of the author of the Gospel depended not on his own developed speculations about the nature of his Master, but on what his Master was and, granted that He was the Word made flesh, upon the value of His teaching.

If we are to believe his own account of the matter, he had learnt from what that Master had done and said that He was more than man, and he wrote his book to commend this faith to others. In instituting a parallel between his writings and those of Plato, this point is habitually lost sight of. Professor Gardner actually says that the accuracy of detail about places in the writers of the New Testament no more guarantees the accuracy of their report of speeches than Plato's topographical accuracy in the setting of the scene of his dialogues guarantees that the words used in the dialogues were ever uttered. Of course, in one sense, it does not. What it does guarantee in the case of the Platonic dialogues is that Plato was acquainted with Athens, and what such accuracy guarantees in the case of the Gospel narratives is that the Evangelists, or their informants, knew Palestine, and that therefore there is a probability that they were acquainted with our Lord, or could obtain reliable information about Him.

We do not know why it is, but the critics now seem to take it for granted that not only the writers of the Gospels, but also the people for whom they wrote were thoroughly indifferent as to the historical truth of the statements that they made about the acts and words of Christ. They point out that contemporary or earlier historians such as Thucydides or Livy cared

much more about the artistic effect of their writings
than about their historic accuracy, and that Thucydides
in particular expressly informs us that he composed
the speeches which he puts into the mouths of his
historical characters in accordance with what he considered they ought to have said on the particular
occasion. They therefore assume that the Evangelists
did the same, and that nothing else was expected
at the time, or ever ought to have been expected,
from their writings.

" Realising this," says Canon Streeter (p. 370),
" we perceive that the original readers of the Fourth
Gospel would never have supposed that the author
intended the speeches put into the mouth of Christ
to be taken as a verbatim report, or even as a précis
of the actual words spoken by Him on the particular
occasions on which they are represented to have been
delivered. They would not have supposed that the
author meant that the doctrine propounded in these
discourses was verbally identical with what was actually
taught by Christ in Palestine, but rather that it was
organically related to what Christ taught in such a
way as to be the doctrine which Christ would have
taught had He been explicitly dealing with the problems confronting the Church at the time the Gospel
was written."

Again he says : " A critical historian should,
unless the contrary be proved, assume that the speeches
in Acts are Thucydidean, and are to be understood
in the same way as the speeches in any contemporary
historian—that is to say, though they are written in
character, their real purpose is to afford the historian
an opportunity for inculcating ideas which he himself
wishes to express. . . . The theology underlying the
speeches in Acts . . . should be read as a presentation
of Luke's own theology " (p. 555).

We venture to think that in this case also no complete parallel can be made out. In the first place, the writers of the Gospels and many of their readers were Jews,* or at least Orientals and not pure Greeks. Canon Streeter allows that the Jewish custom was to collect the *ipsissima verba* of famous teachers, but supposes without any proof that the Fourth Evangelist was influenced by Greek literary models. In the second place, the Gospels were, if we except the Gospel of Luke, written by plain men for plain men.

They were also written by men who had seen their best friends put to death for professing faith in Christ, and who were in danger of death themselves on the same charge for men whose lives were also in jeopardy. It mattered nothing to Thucydides or his readers if the Funeral Oration of Pericles was a " free composition by the writer himself," or contained a condensed account of what Pericles actually said. But we submit that it did matter to John and to the people of Ephesus whether Jesus said, or did not say, " I am the resurrection and the life," and, " He that hath seen Me hath seen the Father." If the people of Ephesus had been so indifferent as to whether the Gospel was a genuine record of the words of Christ from the pen of an eyewitness, why did they add the last two verses ? Why did the writer so strongly insist that he had seen the blood and water come forth from the side of the Lord, and why did he begin his Epistle with so solemn a statement that he was declaring what he had seen with his eyes, what he had beheld and his hands had handled, of the Word of Life ?

It is surely plain from these passages, if there is any meaning in words at all, that the writer of these books at least wished his readers to believe that he was a literal eyewitness of what he recorded, and that

* See Scott Holland, *The Fourth Gospel*, pp. 173, 174.

they expected such attestation from him. He, of course, may have been deceiving them, whether intentionally or not, but we cannot believe that *they* did not suppose that he was giving them at least a précis of what Christ said and a true account of what He did.*

The discourses in the Fourth Gospel have not any special suitability to the circumstances of the Church in Ephesus in the first century, except so far as they have a proved suitability to the circumstances of the Church at all times of its history. How a writer who wrote only with the needs of the Church at that time in a particular part of Asia in mind came to write a book which has been the inspiration of the greatest minds ever since is inexplicable, unless we bring in the inspiration of the Holy Spirit. This some of our English critics are willing to do, including Canon Streeter and Dean Inge. But if one once begins to bring in supernatural influences of this kind, where is one to stop ?

Renan, whose methods of criticism did not differ in any great degree from those employed by the majority of modern critics, said that if miracle and the inspiration of certain books were realities, the methods that he employed were detestable.

To bring in supernatural assistance in support of a critical theory is a strange way of making the origin of the Gospel intelligible and intellectually acceptable

---

* If the people of Ephesus never supposed that the speeches of Christ reported in the Fourth Gospel contained His actual words, or even a précis of them, why was it necessary for the " Elder " to defend the credit of his Gospel by attacking the trustworthiness of Mark and Matthew (pp. 19 *sqq.*) ? Could he not have pointed out to the simple souls who were upset by his novel teaching that he was only giving them what they might reasonably expect, and in fact did expect from him—the doctrine which Christ would have taught if He had been confronted with the problems that faced them ?

to the "modern mind." Surely it is more reverent and more consonant with what we know of the working of God to suppose that the Spirit brought to the mind of the writer what Christ had actually said (as indeed the writer makes Christ promise that He should) than that He inspired the writer in some way or other to state that Christ had said what he (the writer) knew perfectly well that He had not said. The most fashionable way out of this difficulty at the moment is to suggest that the writer imagined that he was an inspired prophet and that he was so confused by his visions that he did not know which of his thoughts about Christ was due to recollection and which was due to ecstasy.

We are told that the writer was a " Christocentric mystic " and that St. Paul was one also ; so, we presume, was the author of the *Imitatio Christi*. We know what sort of writings St. Paul produced under the supposed influence of his mysticism. He at any rate put no words into the mouth of Christ. It is true that the author of the *Imitatio* put many words into the mouth of Christ, but how different is the impression that we receive from his book from that which we receive from the Fourth Gospel !

The author of the Apocalypse was a visionary and claimed to be a prophet, yet he imagined no new incidents in the life of Christ. It is true that he recorded messages which purported to be what Christ said to the Churches of Asia in view of the circumstances of the times, but these messages are quite different from the discourses of the Fourth Gospel, with their obvious suitability to their Jewish background and their universal applicability.

Moreover, the author of the Fourth Gospel himself has left us a treatise in which he adapts the teaching of Christ to his own time—namely, his First Epistle.

How could the men of those days have failed to perceive the difference between the Evangelist's treatment of the words of Christ in the Gospel and in the Epistle ? How could they have failed to suppose that he intended on the whole to convey to them in the Gospel the teaching that Christ actually did give ? At any rate it is certain that every early Church writer who did receive the Gospel treated it as an historical and reliable record of the life and words of Christ while He was on earth.

If the Fourth Gospel is the work of a Christocentric mystic and seer, writing what he supposed to be " a systematic summary of Christian teaching " (*op. cit.*, p. 371) suitable to the times in which he lived, in the form of a Gospel, then we must regard this work as absolutely unique, for it in no way resembles the work of other men of those or other times who may be classed as mystics, seers, or evangelists. Whether it is necessary or scientific to postulate such literary and spiritual novelties without the least precedent, we leave it to our readers to decide.

*   *   *   *   *

It may fairly be objected that the dissertations in this book are mainly negative and critical and do little to deal in a positive way with the well-known difficulties that keep so many people who are professed Christians from believing in the apostolic authorship of the Gospel. In reply to this objection it may be answered that we are dealing with the situation as we find it. At the present moment the fable about the martyrdom of John, the son of Zebedee, has an extraordinary vogue. It has been popularised in England by the efforts of Dr. Moffatt and Dr. Charles, and Dean Inge has given it his blessing. Consequently many writers of less note accept without question the account which these distinguished critics have given of the matter. It was therefore necessary first to clear away this obstacle, which is an absolute bar to the apostolic authorship and is highly valued as such.

Canon Streeter's book is so typical of the present method of dealing with evidence and of the self-contradictions to which modern criticism will resort to get rid of any close connection between the Apostles and the Fourth Gospel, that we have thought it well to deal with it at what may seem, at first sight, disproportionate length.

We have seen into what a morass of improbabilities this writer is led by trying to attribute the Gospel to the " Elder," while at the same time endeavouring to make the connection between the " Elder " and the Beloved Disciple as slight as possible and supposing that the " Elder " only just saw Christ. A theory that requires to be supported by so much ingenious and self-contradictory re-writing of history and so many paradoxes cannot be regarded as probable.

The present position with regard to the authorship of the Gospel may be summarised thus :

(1) Practically all critics admit that the Gospel was written about A.D. 100.

(2) Some admit that it was written by a Jew who was in some way connected with the Apostles, or at least with the first generation of Christians.

(3) The prevalent opinion among many of the more conservative critics is that the Gospel was written by a man who, although not among the number of the Twelve, might yet be called in the fullest sense of the word a Disciple of the Lord and even the Beloved Disciple.

Those who adopt this position do not seem to be influenced by the objection which induces the holders of the second position to deny that the Gospel was written by an actual follower of our Lord, namely,

that it is incredible that one who had known the man
Jesus after the flesh could have written of Him as the
Fourth Evangelist does. By disregarding this objection, those who believe that the Gospel was written
by a personal disciple range themselves on the side of
those who believe that it was written by an Apostle in
all essential particulars.

Although this position has been mentioned and
criticised before in this book, it seems desirable to
gather together the arguments on which it is based,
and to try to estimate their value in their entirety.

These arguments are as follows :

(1) If the Evangelist had been one of the Twelve,
he would not have spoken of himself as the " Beloved
Disciple," while another disciple, outside the number
of the Twelve, might with perfect propriety refer to
one of the Twelve as such.

(2) John, the son of Zebedee, had not the education
and training which would have fitted him to write
such a book as the Fourth Gospel.

(3) His character, as described by the Synoptists,
does not seem suitable to the author of such books as
the Gospel and the First Epistle.

(4) It is difficult to understand how the son of a
Galilean fisherman was " known to the High Priest "
and able to gain admission to his house on an important
occasion.

(5) It is unlikely that he had a house in Jerusalem.

(6) His lack of interest in the Galilean ministry,
and his concentration on the Judean ministry, are best
explained by supposing that he was not with the Lord
in Galilee, but only in Jerusalem.

As for the first of these arguments, we do not
suppose that it would ever have been thought of except
by a school of criticism that is pledged to deny the

apostolic authorship of the Gospel at all costs.   If
it was true that John was the Beloved Disciple of the
Lord, there was no more arrogance in his recording
this fact than there was in St. Paul when he wrote that
it had pleased God to call him by His grace and to
reveal His Son in him.

If the Evangelist had made himself prominent in
the Gospel, or made a display of the reasons why Christ
had so distinguished him, some accusation of pride
might be brought against him.   But this is not the
case ;   the matter is mentioned quite incidentally, just
as any man might casually mention in conversation
that he was his father's favourite son.

Even if we grant for the sake of argument that
there is some trace of perfectly legitimate pride in the
mention of this fact, yet it should be remembered that,
especially on critical principles, even Evangelists are
but men.   Old-fashioned people who believe in inspiration and other uncritical ideas, and who sub-
consciously have the opinion that not only must the
Gospels be infallible but also their authors must be
immaculate, might be excused if they found a difficulty
here.   Yet, strangely enough, they have never done
so.   It is the strong-minded critic who has outgrown
all these opinions, and who does not scruple to attribute
all manner of " free handling " of materials to the
writers of the Gospels, who is so upset by this display
of a little natural human feeling on the part of an
Evangelist, that he regards it as a positive proof that
the man who committed the enormity of stating that
he was the Beloved Disciple could not possibly be an
Apostle.

The second and third of these arguments we think
that we have already sufficiently answered.

As for the fourth, we do not know enough of the
circumstances and relationships of the family of

Zebedee to base any definite conclusion on such an objection.*

As for the fifth, the same remark applies, and it is not certain whether the verse on which the objection is based means that John had a house in Jerusalem.

As for the sixth, the stress that the Evangelist lays on the Judean ministry may just as well be accounted for by the plan of his work which was not intended to cover the ground already covered by the Synoptists.

We do not therefore think that any of the above-mentioned objections are in any way decisive against the attribution of the Gospel to the Apostle. In fact, we altogether fail to see the attractiveness of the theory which would attribute the authorship of the Gospel to an actual disciple of Christ outside the number of the Twelve. We can understand the difficulties that men of a certain philosophic standpoint feel in attributing the Gospel to a man who had known Christ after the flesh, but these half measures seem to serve no other purpose except to keep those who accept them outside the circle of those who are conservative enough to believe in the apostolic authorship of the Gospel and to disregard the jibes that are aimed at their incompetency by those "who believe themselves entitled to speak in the name of criticism."

We feel, therefore, that the main issue of the controversy is still between those who believe that the Gospel was written by John the Apostle, and those who believe that an Apostle could not possibly have produced such a work.

* Renan deals with this passage characteristically:
"Les détails du v. 16 sont d'une étonnante verité. Loin d'y voir une invraisemblance, j'y vois une marque de naïveté, comme celle d'un provinçal qui se vante d'avoir du credit dans un ministère parce qu'il y connaît un concièrge ou un domestique" (*Vie de Jésus*, p. 522).

Many of those who belong to the latter class reject the apostolic authorship of the book frankly on account of their attitude towards the supernatural. Renan says that the question of the supernatural lies at the bottom of all discussions of such subjects, and that it is evident that the Gospels are legendary in parts, because they are full of accounts of miracles.

Dr. Reynolds states the position of such critics very concisely when he writes : " A philosophy based on the intrinsic unknowableness of God and on the impossibility of converse being held between man and his Creator is pledged to demonstrate the late origin of the Fourth Gospel and to find in the Johannine teaching of St. Paul some of the materials of this *falsarius* of the second century " (Hastings, *Dictionary of Bible*, II. 694).

Long ago Strauss wrote that the Gospel history would be irrefutable if it was certain that it had been written by eyewitnesses, or by men who lived near the time of the supposed events. Consequently for a long time the efforts of the unbelieving school of criticism were concentrated on the endeavour to ascribe the Gospels to as late a date as possible. These efforts are not now regarded as having been successful. At the present time it is generally admitted that the Epistles of St. Paul were written between 49 and 61. That a very early Jerusalem tradition, if not the recollections of St. Peter himself, stand behind the Gospel of St. Mark. That St. Luke was a companion of St. Paul and wrote the Gospel and the Acts at least before A.D. 80, and that even the Fourth Gospel cannot be dated later than A.D. 110. According to the statement by Strauss, quoted above, these admissions should be enough to make it reasonable to believe that the Gospel story is generally reliable.

We do not, however, find that our modern critics

who have been compelled to attribute so much of the New Testament to writers contemporary, or nearly contemporary, with the events that it records are any more inclined to believe in the possibility of the supernatural than their predecessors. They still rely on a modified form of Strauss' mythopoetic theory, which may be briefly described in the words of Renan : " A rapid process of transformation took place in the twenty or thirty years which followed the death of Jesus and imposed on His biography the absolute forms of an ideal legend."

But whereas Strauss and his early followers required a long time for the growth of the legends about Jesus which were supposed to be recorded in the Gospels, the modern school of criticism is obliged to be content with a comparatively short time and to imagine that these legends grew up with unprecedented rapidity.

Now, it is obvious that if any theory of the origin of the Gospels that involves the recognition of the possibility of the supernatural is either rejected as *a priori* impossible, or quietly ignored, any other theory that does not involve the supernatural must be regarded as more probable, no matter how far it may contradict all reasonable probability and all human experience.

Therefore, to those who, whether explicitly or not, have made up their minds that any explanation of the origin of, let us say the Fourth Gospel, which involves the supposition that it may contain a generally historical account of One who claimed to be and actually was the Son of God is quite impossible, any other theory, however wildly improbable, must be preferable.

Many have persuaded themselves that there was time between the death of Christ and the end of the first century for the figure of the historical Jesus to

have receded so far into the background as to make
it possible for the spiritual experiences of some of
His followers who had never really seen Him in the
flesh to produce an idealised picture of His person
and teaching such as that which we find in the Fourth
Gospel. This gets rid of the historical character of
some part of the picture of Christ which the New
Testament as a whole presents to us. But much that
is very disconcerting remains, even in the Synoptic
Gospels. It is found to be necessary to push the process of idealisation and legend-making much farther
back, if the existence of the New Testament is to be
acounted for on rational principles.

Although it is said that the Synoptists survived
not so much as a record of " Church theology " as in
spite of it, they need a thorough expurgation before
those who think that they have discredited the Fourth
Gospel with comparative ease can rest quietly in the
assurance that they have rewritten the story of Jesus
in such a way that it may fairly be called " historical "
in the narrow modern sense of the word.*

It is interesting to see how much a thorough-going
Modernist like Loisy thinks it necessary to remove before
the Gospel story is reduced to a reasonable condition.
He is willing to allow † that Jesus believed Himself
to be the Messiah in a more spiritual sense than was
usual with those who laid claim to this position. However, He only declared Himself to be such towards
the end of His ministry, and then only to His disciples.
He went to Jerusalem either with the intention of
declaring Himself there, or with the hope that He
would be revealed as such by the divine manifestation

---

* How narrow this view is may be judged from the words of
Loisy: "L'historien n'a pas à s'inspirer de l'agnosticisme pour
écarter Dieu de l'histoire. Il ne l'y recontre jamais."

† Loisy, *Les Evangiles Syn., passim.*

K

of the Kingdom. Until this was revealed, He was not in the full sense of the term the Messiah, but only the Messiah-elect. He also believed that He was the Son of God, but only in the sense in which all men are sons of God, though possibly in a higher degree. He did not go to Jerusalem with the intention of dying there, but only to prepare and procure, at the risk of His life, the coming of the Kingdom of God. The obstacles that He had met with in His career as a teacher made Him foresee vaguely and at intervals the probability that the Messiah could not enter into His glory, except by passing through death. After the success of His triumphal entry and His dispute with the religious leaders, the situation became such that it could not be unravelled except by a miracle, or a catastrophe. It was the catastrophe that happened, although to the last Jesus never ceased to hope for the miracle. He regarded death as a risk that must be run, but not as an element necessary in itself of His messianic function, or as a saving act on which all the future depended.

This, according to Loisy, is a summary of the true history of Jesus. Everything in the Gospels which contradicts this simple and natural story is the work of Christian tradition, the product of faith, or of primitive apologetics.

Consequently, the saying, " No man knoweth the Son but the Father, neither knoweth any man the Father save the Son," cannot be genuine, but betrays the faith of the Christian community.

Even the passage, " But of that day and that hour knoweth no man, no, not the angels which are in heaven, neither the Son, but the Father," must be considered to have been interpolated by tradition or the Evangelist. " In the circumstances of the Evangelical preaching the simple assertion of the secret of the Father ought to have been enough, and the absolute use of the word Son to designate the Saviour does not belong to the language of Jesus, nor to that of primitive Evangelical tradition. If it had not been added by the Evangelist, the whole passage would become suspect."

The Parable of the Vineyard must also go, because in it Jesus is represented as speaking of Himself as the Son in an absolute sense. In the passage about the confession of Peter, the Evangelist is responsible for the antithesis between the Son of Man in the question of Jesus and the Son of God in the reply of Peter.

As Jesus never claimed to remit sins by His own authority, the story of the paralytic at Capernaum, and the sinful woman at the Pharisee's feast, have obviously been glossed by the Evangelists in the interests of a later theology.

The description of the Last Judgment in Matthew xxv. 31, must have been imagined by the Evangelist himself, as Jesus never expected that He would be the Judge of the living and the dead.

The scene of the trial before Caiaphas is also due to Christian tradition, because it represents Jesus as being condemned for blasphemy, since He said that He was the Son of God.

It is much easier to explain this on the ground that it is congruous with the theology of Mark and Matthew than by its historical probability. The members of the Sanhedrin are said to have agreed with Caiaphas on the question of blasphemy and to have condemned Jesus to death in accordance with the law of Leviticus. But, in accordance with that law, the blasphemer ought to have been stoned. But Jesus was crucified, and suffered this punishment after a regular trial by the Roman authority, where the accusation was not blasphemy against God for

assuming divine prerogatives, but messianic claims to
the Kingdom of Israel. The trial before the Sanhedrin was therefore entirely due to the imagination
of Christian tradition, in order to transfer the responsibility of the condemnation of Jesus from the
Roman authority to the Jews.

Lastly, after the death of Jesus, His body was
thrown into the common pit where criminals were
buried and could therefore not be produced by the
Jews when the Disciples put out the story of the
resurrection, as it would by that time have been
impossible to identify it. The whole story of the
burial and the empty tomb is "controversial
expedient."

"The burial has no interest except with regard
to the resurrection. In order to prove that Jesus rose
from the tomb, it is first necessary to show that He
was put there. Now, He could not have been put
there by His disciples, because the body was not at
their disposition. The intervention of an important
personage was therefore necessary. The one that
Mark mentions is otherwise unknown to apostolic
tradition; the other details of the burial serve to explain the action of the women and the discovery of
the empty tomb on the Sunday morning."

With regard to this last brilliant specimen of
"historical criticism" it is sufficient to say that by
Roman Law (*Digest*, xlviii.) the bodies of criminals
must be given up to any one who asked for them, and
therefore there is no reason whatever why the body
of Jesus should not have been buried by His disciples.
It is quite untrue to say that Joseph of Arimathea
"is otherwise unknown to apostolic tradition," as he
is mentioned in the three other Gospels, and even if
he were not, the fact that he would in that case be
only mentioned in the Gospel which all critics unite

in considering to be the primary authority for the life of Christ would be no proof whatever that he was not an historical person.

If Jesus was nothing but the harmless fanatic which critics of this school would see in Him, it is obvious that His followers must have been remarkable men to have produced the Figure that has admittedly wrought the greatest moral reformation that the world has ever known, and that so many great and wise men have worshipped as their Lord and Master, out of such poor material.

Let us hear how they did it. " We must not represent the work of Christian thought as an effort to distort history for the benefit of abstract opinions. It was the opinions that were swept away in the movement of faith. Paul and the other theologians of the first age were strangers to scientific research and even to philosophic reflection. They had their intuitions which took them off their feet ; their theories were visions. . . . In the state of exaltation in which the first believers lived all this process which defies analysis by its complexity spontaneously and rapidly operated in that subconscious region of the soul where come into being the dreams of all men and, in the case of some, hallucinations and the intuitions of genius. One cannot doubt that certain words attributed to Christ were present in the minds of these enthusiasts in the transports of their ecstatic prayers. One can say the same of certain stories of miracles, and up to a certain point for all of them the involuntary transformation of recollections in the believing imagination was a kind of vision " (Loisy, *op. cit.*, vol. i., p. 194).

Most people who have not definitely made up their minds to exclude the possibility that the Gospel history can have had any supernatural cause will feel that the obscurity of the language in which this explanation of its origin is given is the measure of the improbability of explanations of this kind.

Yet this is the type of explanation upon which the most modern critics seem to rely. They seem to have come to the conclusion that if Christ is allowed to have had any real part in the production and formation of Christian theology, as it appears in the completed New Testament, they will be in great danger of being forced to admit that He was a supernatural Person. They shrink from Renan's hypothesis that there was some kind of connivance between Christ and the Apostles in the production of the myths concerning Him, and they throw the whole responsibility for the production of everything that goes beyond the simple story of an unhappy religious genius, such as that quoted from Loisy above, upon the first preachers of Christianity, crediting them at the same time with a type of hallucination and spiritual exaltation which, to say the least of it, is somewhat unusual. The explanation which Loisy gives of the origin of the Synoptic Gospels is exactly the same as that by means of which Canon Streeter and others would account for the Fourth Gospel. Even the Gospel of Mark is regarded by the most advanced critics as " Pauline " and far from historical.

If it is reasonable to imagine that a person endowed with the very peculiar type of mystic experience with which the Fourth Evangelist is now credited was able to write that Gospel, then the description of the origin of the Synoptic Gospels given above cannot be at once rejected as absurd.

If, on the other hand, it is felt that to try to account for the Synoptic Gospels in this way passes all reasonable credibility, then it follows that those who are trying to account for the Fourth Gospel in a similar way are not on very secure ground.

It is true that before the Fourth Gospel was written there was more time for the mythopoetic process to work, but the difference in time is not very great, and there is no evidence at all that the people who lived at the end of the first century were more indifferent to historical truth than those who lived in the middle of the century. St. Luke, in order to secure a favourable reception for his book, promised to give his readers " certainty " about the things in which they had been instructed, and there is nothing in the Fourth Gospel to show that the expectations with which its readers would approach it differed in any way from those of the readers of the Third Gospel. For those who still have an open mind with regard to the question of the supernatural, the whole method of accounting for the origin of the Gospels which we have been discussing would seem to be a mistake. It was avowedly produced by its authors to account for the Gospels without making allowance for the existence of the supernatural in any form.

It must of necessity start with the supposition that Jesus was a mere man : it is forced in the end to admit that the Apostles must have been more than men, for they produced quite unconsciously out of their confused recollections of a Jewish workman something that blended so well with the orgiastic cults of the period, that it not only produced the highest system of morality that the world has ever known, but also possessed a strange and hitherto unexampled power which enabled men to live up to the claims of this morality, and did this not only for the cultured and leisured philosophic class, but also, and indeed most frequently, for the weakest and most down-trodden members of the human race.

Those who do not believe in the supernatural may explain this paradox as they please ; but why should those who believe that Jesus was a Divine Person adopt their methods and expect that they will lead them into all truth ?

We believe that the battle of New Testament criticism will have to be fought out in the end, not in the Johannine question, but in the Synoptic problem. If the Synoptic Gospels should be finally discredited from an historical point of view, it will be a waste of time to argue about the apostolic authorship and historical character of the Fourth Gospel, for if one body of visionary fanatics could have produced the first three Gospels, another rather more remarkable visionary fanatic might have produced the Fourth.

Conversely, if we grant that a Christocentric mystic, or a seer, or call him what name you will, could have produced the Fourth Gospel on little or no historical basis, we shall have gone a long way towards admitting that it is possible for similar persons to have produced those parts of the other three which are offensive to the supposed demands of the " stern historical method."

But if, on the other hand, the conflict ends in establishing the whole of the Synoptic portrait of Jesus as substantially historical, and if it be allowed, as indeed it must be, that the Pauline Epistles were produced concurrently with, if not before, the first three Gospels, then it will require a good deal of perversity to maintain that the delineation of Jesus in the Fourth Gospel cannot be by the hand of an Apostle simply because it makes Him lay too explicit claim to divinity in the fullest sense of the term.

The difficulties that will then remain to be dealt with lie more in the manner of the presentation of the history and claims of Jesus in the Fourth Gospel and in the contrast which this offers to the Synoptic

account, than in the question as to whether He did
claim in the clearest possible language that those
that had seen Him had seen the Father.

That such difficulties exist no reasonable person
will deny. For example, it is pointed out that in the
Synoptic Gospels Jesus is represented as revealing His
messianic dignity very gradually and checking those
who were desirous of making Him known before He
wished it.

His teaching in these Gospels, it is said, lays stress
on morality and trust in God, while His most severe
denunciations are reserved for the hypocritical and
immoral. In the Fourth Gospel He is represented as
turning the thoughts of His hearers to His Person
from the beginning of His ministry and stating His
claim to be the Messiah and the Son of God in a unique
sense in the most unequivocal language. Moreover,
according to a recent writer,* " His voice is heard in
continual angry contest " with the Jews. This is, of
course, a gross exaggeration, but it cannot be denied
that the Fourth Evangelist does at times attribute
to our Lord very plain speaking with regard to those
who are wilfully deaf to His claims. We must remember, however, that the Synoptists chiefly present Him in His relations with the fanatical people of
Galilee, who were only too ready to accept Him at
their own valuation and to make Him a king by force.
In the only scene in which the Fourth Evangelist
shows Him in contact with the people of Galilee He
shows exactly the same reluctance to commit Himself to their enthusiasm as He shows in the Synoptic
story. It must also be noted that the two most
explicit declarations that He is represented as making
with regard to the dignity of His Person, with the
exception of those forced on Him in controversy with

* Lord Charnwood.

the Jews, are made to the Samaritan woman and the blind beggar.

If the Fourth Evangelist had been inventing an imaginary series of incidents to form a background for teaching suitable to the condition of the Church in Ephesus at the end of the first century, what made him choose these two most unlikely and unsuitable persons as the recipients of such teaching ?

If, however, these incidents are true, what could be more in keeping with the method and mind of the Jesus of the Synoptists, who ate with publicans and sinners, and who thanked His Father that He had hidden the deep things of the Gospel from the wise and prudent and revealed them to babes ? Who among the philosophically minded Jewish Christians of Ephesus was likely to have invented this subtle coincidence ?

There is an incident recorded in the Gospel which seems in every way suitable for introducing some message fitted for those whom the Evangelist is supposed to have specially had in mind in the composition of his Gospel : we mean the incident of the Greeks who came desiring to see Jesus. What an opportunity to put into the mouth of Jesus some discourse which would have settled all the theological difficulties that were agitating the Christian Greeks of Ephesus, of which Canon Streeter has drawn such a vivid picture !

But the Evangelist makes no use of this incident in the way that we should have expected ; he never even mentions whether the Greeks were introduced to our Lord, or not.

As for the statements about His Person made in the course of His controversy with the Jews, it is only reasonable to suppose that our Lord may have spoken plainly to the religious leaders of the people who were so little likely to take Him as their king by force, that they even doubted if He was a good man at all, in order that they might have the opportunity of knowing what he really claimed to be, and so be without excuse if they rejected Him.

It is obvious that the Evangelist has only recorded the general outline of these discourses to the Jews, and has also largely recast them into his own diction.

Those who are not tied to the theory of the mechanical inspiration of Scripture can have no reason to deny that the temperament of the writers of the various books of the New Testament has influenced their presentation of the facts that they have to relate and the thoughts which they express.

The writers of the Synoptic Gospels have described to us the passionate and strenuous temperament with which the " Son of Thunder " entered upon his career as a disciple, and traces of it are still visible in the stories that are told of his later years and in the manner in which he denounces the adversaries of the truth in his Epistles and in the absolute contrast that he there draws between the world and God.   It is therefore reasonable to suppose that he may have sharpened the edge of some of the sayings that he has attributed to our Lord in His controversy with the Jews, and this is a partial answer to the objection that these discourses are not in keeping with the character which the Jesus of the Synoptists is popularly supposed to have possessed.   Moreover, it should not be forgotten how much of sternness there is in the character of the Synoptic Jesus, how overwhelming are the demands which He is represented as making on His followers, and what absolute devotion to His Person and cause He claims from them.

It is, of course, easy to dismiss all this as " Church theology," although it is contrary to all that we know of human nature to suppose that men, even if they were liable to ecstatic visions, should deliberately make the way of salvation so MORALLY difficult.

It is certain, at any rate, that in these days this sterner side of the Gospel is very generally kept out of sight, and, if faithfully presented, causes offence. The theology of many of us may be summed up in the words of the Persian Epicurean :

"He's a good fellow : and 'twill all be well."

It is therefore only natural that the bluntness with which the Fourth Evangelist has recorded our Lord's teaching about the danger of refusing to accept Him should shock the susceptible ears of many. If Jesus Christ is what He is represented as claiming to be in the Fourth Gospel, and if it is true that only self-righteousness, self-will and unrepented sin keep men from admitting His claims, when they are fairly put before them, then surely He was more than justified in putting the alternatives of faith and unbelief plainly before His hearers, if they were persons who were fitted by their circumstances and training to profit by such teaching.

This argument will, of course, have no weight with those who believe that the " Johannine theology " is nothing more than the pious opinion of certain members of the early Church ; it is not addressed to them.

The other apparent discrepancies between the Fourth Gospel and the Synoptists have been dealt with in many books, and more or less satisfactory explanations have been given of them. It is not proposed to go over this ground again here.

The author is convinced that, however formidable they may be, there is one greater difficulty still to be explained by those who will not allow the Fourth

Gospel to have been the work of an eyewitness of the life of Christ, and that is how a stream can rise higher than its source.

Why is it reasonable to suppose that Jesus was an altogether unique person—which is admitted by all critics whose theories have gained any general accept-ance—and then to attribute that part of His Gospel which has been most potent for good, and which has been the stay of all His Saints, not to Himself, but to the visions, the ecstasies, or, at the best, to the spiritual experience of His followers ?

How is it that Gospel-making, which seems to be regarded as such a normal and natural function of the human mind that it arouses no suspicion or repugnance in the minds of the straitest sect of the anti-super-naturalists, came to an abrupt end at the death of the author of the Fourth Gospel and was immediately followed by a period singularly lacking in originality, when the only thing possible to Christian experience seems to have been to comment and meditate on what had been already written ?

Some say that this unfortunate result was due to the formation of the Canon as a bulwark against heresy, and so this authorised romancing came to an end.   Is this really convincing ?

Is not the more simple explanation likely to be the true one, namely, that, since all those who had " seen the Lord " had passed away, no one was ever again able to write a Gospel which commended itself to the Church as a worthy portrait of its Founder ?

ADDITIONAL NOTES

To last line but one, page 62.

Bishop Lightfoot, on the other hand, wrote, " If then the genuineness of this Gospel is supported by greater evidence than in ordinary cases we consider conclusive, we approach the investigation of its internal character with a very strong presupposition in its favour. The ONUS PROBANDI rests with those who impugn its genuineness, and nothing short of the fullest and most decisive marks of spuriousness can fairly be considered sufficient to counterbalance the evidence " (*Biblical Essays*, p. 10). We can only presume that Dr. Streeter classes Bishop Lightfoot among critics who do not know their business.

Line 26, page 124.

Bishop Lightfoot points out in his *Biblical Essays*, pp. 11–13, how the Fourth Evangelist avoids dealing with the very questions which would interest the Church of Ephesus at the time when the Gospel was written, namely, the divine origin of the episcopate, the Gnostic doctrine of emanations, the time for celebrating Easter.

Line 9, page 73.

Dr. Sanday in his pre-Modernist days found no difficulty in the fact that St. John should call himself the " Beloved Disciple." He says, " There is nothing unnatural in this ; it is a little complex perhaps, but only with the complexity of life, when different motives clash in a fine nature. The delicacy of attitude corresponds to an innate delicacy of mind. When one reads some of the criticisms of this attitude, one is reminded of a sentence in an English classic. Cowper's indignant remonstrance at Johnson's treatment of Milton :

" As a poet he has treated him with severity enough, and has plucked one or two of the most beautiful feathers out of his Muse's wing and trampled them under his great foot ! " (*The Criticism of the Fourth Gospel*, p. 80).

This shows how completely subjective and worthless this sort of criticism is.

RECENT CRITICISM OF THE GOSPEL

SINCE this book was first published several studies on the Fourth Gospel have appeared. Their general tendency has been to retreat from the extreme position that the Gosepl is an allegorical romance, but on the whole there has been no inclination to accept the Apostle as the actual author, although a very near approach has been made to this. Archbishop Bernard in his commentary would regard the Apostle as the source of the matter contained in the Gospel, but the " Elder " as his amanuensis who put the matter into shape. His argument is as follows. In second-century writers the term " Apostle " stands primarily for the Twelve, although it is also applied to St. Paul. The distinguishing feature of an Apostle is that he is one who has seen the Lord.

The term " Presbyter " is applied to those who carried on the work of the Apostles. This is clearly seen in Acts xv. 4 and 22. Irenæus uses the term in the same sense. He writes, " Wherefore we ought to obey the Presbyters who are in the churches, those who have succession from the Apostles " (*Adv. Hær*. iv. 26, 2). And again, " The Presbyters, the disciples of the Apostles." Dr. Bernard therefore assumes that the word Presbyter or Elder means in Irenæus those " who whether officially or unofficially had succeeded to the position of leadership which the Apostles held " (*Commentary on St. John*, vol. i., p. xlvi.). He believes that, when Irenæus speaks of " John the Disciple of the Lord," he means the son of Zebedee, and that he makes no attempt to distinguish between two Johns (*op. cit.* p. xlviii.). He also thinks that it is difficult to believe that Irenæus could have misunderstood what he heard from Polycarp about John.

He thus rejects all the theories of Harnack, Burney, Streeter, Wellhausen and Schwartz to which reference has been made in this book.

He sums up the matter as follows : " Irenæus, then, only knows of one John at Ephesus, whom he speaks of as John the Beloved Disciple and an Apostle ; he regards him as the author of the Gospel and the Apocalypse as well as of Epistles i. and ii." (*op. cit.* p. xlix.). This would seem to settle the question in favour of the apostolic authorship of the Gospel, but it does not. Dr. Bernard is so convinced that the term Presbyter or Elder is a technical term for Christians of the generation immediately after the Apostles, that the mere fact that the writer of the Second Epistle calls himself " the Elder " proves that he was not the Apostle. As Dr. Bernard believes that this Epistle is from the same hand as the Gospel, it follows that the Apostle cannot have been the author of the Gospel. He urges in support of this argument that " there is no example in the literature of the second century of the equation Elder equals Apostle " (p. xlvii.). Yet Irenæus, on Dr. Bernard's own admission, accepted the Second Epistle where the author calls himself the Elder as being the work of the author of the Gospel who was, in his opinion, an Apostle. Who is likely to be a better judge of the meaning of a technical word, a man living at the time when, and in the place where, it is supposed to have been used, or an Archbishop of Dublin in the twentieth century ?

Moreover, as we have already pointed out, the title " Fellow-Elder " is used by the author of the

Epistle attributed to St. Peter. Dr. Bernard brushes this fact on one side with the remark that it is not really an exception to his statement. But this is not argument.

Canon Streeter, on the other hand, was so troubled by the presence of this expression in an Epistle attributed to St. Peter that he gets over the difficulty by attributing the Epistle to Aristion, " frankly as a guess—but, I hope, a scientific guess " (*The Primitive Church*, p. 130).

We have already pointed out that the word Presbyter is a neutral word and takes its meaning from its context. It is used in the Old Testament of the Elders of the Jews. The writer of the Epistle to the Hebrews uses it of the worthies of Israel (Heb. xi. 2).

In the New Testament generally, and in the writings of the Apostolic Fathers, it is used of the officials whom the Apostles appointed in Jerusalem and also in the churches of the Gentiles. By the time the Pastoral Epistles were written this meaning was well established and there is no reason to think that the meaning of the word was afterwards widened to include ALL who, whether officially or UNOFFICIALLY, had succeeded to the position of leadership which the Apostles held, as Dr. Bernard would have us believe.

If John the Apostle wrote the Apocalypse and described himself there as " John your brother," it does not seem impossible that in a place, where he was the head of the official ministers of the Church, he should have described himself as " the Elder " in a private letter, especially as he seems to have preferred to speak of himself by an impersonal title. The fact that a personal name is used in the Apocalypse is in accordance with the literary convention with regard to this sort of writing.

L

When Dr. Bernard comes to deal with the statement in John xxi. 24 that the Beloved Disciple " beareth witness about these things and WROTE these things," he allows that the present tense " witnesseth " may imply that the Apostle was alive when these words were added to the Gospel and that the words " these things " refer to the whole content of the Gospel.

He then adds : " ὁ γράψας ταῦτα. *Prima facie*, this indicates that the Beloved Disciple actually wrote the Gospel with his own hand, including the appendix, and not only that his reminiscences are behind it. But γράφειν is sometimes used when dictation only is indicated. *E.g.* Pilate wrote a title and put it on the Cross (John xix. 19) means that Pilate was responsible for the wording of the titulus, but hardly that he himself wrote on the wooden board. So Paul says, " I write the more boldly to you " (Rom. xv. 15), while it appears from Rom. xvi. 22 that the scribe of the Epistle was one Tertius (*cf.* Gal. vi. 11 and 1 Pet. v. 12). The Elders of the Church certified that the Beloved Disciple caused these things to be written. *They were put into shape* [italics ours] by the writer who took them down, and afterwards published them, not as his own, but as the Gospel according to John " (*op. cit.* vol. ii., p. 713).

It is surely obvious that the examples that Dr. Bernard selects to prove that γράφειν can be used to mean " dictate " are taken from passages where the context suggests this meaning, with the exception of Gal. vi. 11, where the word seems to mean " write " in the strictest sense, and is generally taken to mean this. Even in the case of Pilate, where the context no more suggests that he wrote the titulus than that he put it on the Cross, we are told that he identified the actual words written with his thoughts. With regard to the Epistle to the Romans, we do not know that it has ever been suggested that Tertius did anything else but write down exactly what the Apostle Paul dictated to him.

Dr. Bernard tells us that the employment of scribes was common. There is no need to dispute this, but that the Apostle John did use a scribe cannot be proved from this passage, still less that this scribe was the " Elder." Even if this worthy ever existed, it cannot be shown that he was ever in Ephesus. The eminent American critic, Dr. Bacon, in an article in the *Hibbert Journal* for January, 1931, demolishes all the evidence that there is supposed to be for the existence of John the Elder at Ephesus and derides the half-Traditionalist writers who will cling to their " Ersatz-Johannes," whom he disrespectfully describes as " a higher-critical myth," not the first of the family, we believe.

He adds, " A carefully considered verdict compels us to state that the much-desired cap-stone to the theory of Dionysius is a higher-critical mare's nest of the purest breed."

Tantæne animis cælestibus iræ? However this may be, we regret to notice that Dr. Bernard, following one of the most fallacious methods of " criticism," first only implies that the Apostle used an amanuensis and then expands the statement into something quite different.

First he says that the Elders of the Church certified that John " caused these things to be written down," a statement which is harmless but unproved, and then says that they " were put into shape " by the man who took them down, which is quite another thing.

This makes the Apostle to be the " witness " behind the Gospel, and the " Elder " to be something decidedly more than his amanuensis.

This theory is supported, as usual, by a reference to John xix. 35, which is far from convincing. The

style of the Gospel is so distinctive and so obviously
the production of a remarkable personality, that we
cannot doubt that a man who wrote like this in
"putting into shape" matter communicated to him
by another person must have interposed a good deal
of his own personality between the Apostle and his
readers. Perhaps this is what is intended. Yet
Dr. Bernard has set himself right across the current of
modern historical criticism in allowing that the Gospel
is in the main historical and that the recollections of an
eye-witness lie immediately behind it. It is strange
indeed, then, when he has gone so far, he should support
a mediating theory of authorship with such uncon-
vincing arguments.

Dr. Stanton, in his first volume on *The Historical
Character of the Gospels*, supported the apostolic authorship with vigour, but in the last volume, written
seventeen years afterwards, he says, "It is further
said of the disciple in question that he 'wrote these
things.' 'These things' can here, at any rate, only
refer to the preceding twenty chapters, if the appendix
was written after his death." He then asks what
exact meaning can be assigned to this statement and
says, "We observe first a certain want of precision
therein ; he says 'these things,' not 'this book.'
Further, the words 'and wrote these things' seem to be
added to 'beareth witness to these things' as a kind
of afterthought. More prominence, at all events, is
given to his having borne witness. From the position
and form of this reference to writing it is not unfair
to infer that there may have been some uncertainty
in the mind of the framer of this statement as to the
extent to which it was to be attributed to the same
disciple " (*op. cit.* vol. iii., p. 133).

It only requires a very elementary knowledge of
Latin and Greek to know how many statements in

these languages "lack precision" through the use of
such words as ταῦτα and "hæc." The exact meaning
of these pronouns is continually left to be understood
from the context. It is true that English authors are
generally more precise, but this does not help Dr.
Stanton's argument. It has no force in this context :
and his second argument that the words "and wrote
these things" are added as an afterthought has less
force still. What can be the value of a theory that
requires this desperate special pleading to commend
it ?

Those who wish to read the last word in perverse
ingenuity in arguing about this subject are referred
to Dr. Garvie's treatment of the last chapter of the
Gospel in the "Abingdon" Bible, and that by the
Rev. R. G. Griffith in his *Gospel History Examined*.

* * * * *

By far the most bold and interesting study of the
Gospel in the last few years is to be found in Professor
Raven's *Jesus and the Gospel of Love*.

Until recently he believed with all members of
his school of thought that the Gospel was a devotional
treatise which did not record factual history about
Jesus, except to a very limited extent. For twelve
years this conviction kept him from writing or saying
much about the book. But he is now convinced that
it is impossible to preach a full Gospel without it and
very reluctantly he has controverted most of the
"critical" positions with regard to it.

He rejects the idea that is to be found in nearly all
modern commentaries on this Gospel, that it does not
matter in the least who wrote it, so long as we learn
the lessons which it is intended to teach. He says,
"If we are to estimate its value, it will make a vast
difference whether the author's personal equation is
the natural result of years of remembrance, or a

sophisticated attempt to accommodate Christianity to philosophy, or to produce a fictitious apologetic, or to construct an esoteric allegory" (*op. cit.* p. 227). If the Gospel is to be regarded as no more than a poem or a devotional rhapsody, it will not " help us to see God expressed in the historic Son of Man" and will leave us "predisposed to exaggerate the difference between the Christ of imagination and the Jesus whose human impact we can trace on St. Mark. Almost we are tempted to surmise that the artist who could produce so superb a revelation must himself be a more sublime spirit than his Master, and that " John" and not Jesus is the revealer to us of God " (*op. cit.* p. 285). Professor Raven describes the figure imagined by Canon Streeter for the Evangelist as " a psychological and moral monstrosity" who outrages our standards of history " by a device which presents to us the products of imagination and religious experience as a record of actual events." He adds that such a writer would be " a traitor to the true interests of Christendom " (*op. cit.* pp. 163, 164).

This is, of course, no more than has been urged in the foregoing pages, but here we have it said by a Regius Professor of Divinity at Cambridge who cannot be dismissed, as the author of this book might be in advanced circles, as a hide-bound and ignorant Traditionalist.

Professor Raven also deals with the thorny question of the difference between the representation of our Lord's teaching in the Synoptists, especially in St. Mark. With regard to the growing consciousness of Messiahship which so many critics have traced in the Second Gospel he says, " It is an exaggeration to represent it as involving a growing consciousness of Messiahship. The development is determined rather by the educational needs of the disciples than by their

Teacher's altered conception of His status" (*op. cit.* p. 215).

Again : "We may trace a development in the exposition, in the form and language under which they [the Messiahship and the Kingdom of God] are presented, but there is no development in the claim made. From His baptism or His first appearance in the Synagogue at Capernaum the character of Jesus shows no sign of change. It is easy to understand why in His teaching in Galilee He delayed the plain statement of His own relationship to God, though that relationship is implicit from first to last. There is nothing in the Synoptic record to make it impossible, or even unlikely, that in Jerusalem and at the festivals He should have spoken more plainly" (*op. cit.* p. 243).

There is much besides in the book on the same general lines as those exemplified in the above quotations. The author comes to the conclusion that the book contains an account of a part of the teaching of Jesus which was passed over by the other Evangelists and that its author may well have been the Apostle John.

The Gospel, he says, is "the story of the author's discipleship, love's memory of love incarnate with the mark of a great devotion writ plainly upon it" (*op. cit.* p. 227).

This conclusion is remarkable indeed as coming from a man who for twelve years abstained from any public attempt to consider the Fourth Gospel, lest the tendency that he felt to regard it as historical should be due to a "wish-fulfilment."

"I have accepted," he says, "the conclusion that in my lifetime those of us who would put truth before tradition must accept the Johannine taboo, and that if they had doubts about it must, for their own credit

and for the better commending of a reasonable faith,
keep these doubts unspoken " (*op. cit.* p. 165).

This attitude of mind which he has at last
abandoned we are glad to see he admits was " not a
very creditable position " (p. 165).

It would have been thought that such a change of
opinion, supported as it is by arguments which we
have had only space to glance at, would have caused
some stirring of the dry bones of " criticism."

But it has only been mentioned in the Modernist
press, as far as we have noticed, with the comment that
Professor Raven does not seem to see the difficulties
which his new opinions involve him in.

It is plain from his book that he sees them all and
has faced them. What is needed from the Modernist
side is not superciliousness about such a book, but
refutation, line by line.

Those of us who have never been misled, but who
have seen the force all along of the arguments which
Professor Raven puts forward with a clearness which
leaves nothing to be desired, can only congratulate
him on his courage, and rejoice that he has the insight
not to be permanently entangled in the sophistications
in which this question has so long been enmeshed.

There is little probability that the truth is on the
side of an argument which requires for its support the
broken reeds of Philip of Side and Georgius, which
invents for the author of the Gospel which has so long
been the heart of the Christian message an author who
is " a psychological and moral monstrosity," which
treats all the authors of the second century as fools
or knaves, and which sets on one side as of no value
a tradition which was common to both the Church and
the heretics immediately after the date when it is
admitted that the Gospel was written.

Inasmuch as this supposedly historical argument

is really based on a theory which depends on a recent conception of the nature of God and the universe which is now passing away and not on any new discoveries in the field of history or literature, it is well to remember the words of Dr. Matthews :

" No idolatry is more absurd than the worship of the modern mind. It is modern thought itself which has taught us to take no age and the mind of no age as final " (*Gospel and the Modern Mind*, p. 31).

INDEX

THE END

PRINTED IN GREAT BRITAIN BY WILLIAM CLOWES AND SONS, LIMITED, LONDON AND BECCLES.

To the Rev. R. E. S. Hodgson

from the

Author